THE
COMPLETE
BOOK OF
PARROTS

THE COMPLETE BOOK OF PARROTS

ROSEMARY LOW

American Consulting Editor
Matthew M. Vriends, PhD

BARRON'S
New York

First edition for the United States published 1989 by
Barron's Educational Series, Inc.
Published 1988 by Merehurst Limited, London, UK.
© Copyright 1988 Merehurst Limited

All inquiries should be addressed to:
Barron's Educational Series, Inc.
250 Wireless Boulevard
Hauppauge, New York 11788

International Standard Book No. 0–8120–5971–9
Library of Congress No.88–24139

Library of Congress Cataloging in Publication Data
Low, Rosemary.
    The complete book of parrots.
    1. Parrots – Dictionaries. I. Vriends, Matthew M., 1937 –   . II. Title.
SF473.P3L678 1989   636.6′865   88–24139
ISBN 0–8120–5971–9

Cover photographs: Front: Sun Conure (main picture)
and Turquoisine Parakeet (inset) (both by
Cyril Laubscher). Back: Blue-crowned
Hanging Parrot (by Rosemary Low).

Editor: Lesley Young
Designer: Carole Perks
Typesetting by Deltatype Ltd, Ellesmere Port, UK
Reprographics by J Film Process Ltd, Bangkok, Thailand
Printed in Portugal by Printer Portuguesa Industria Grafica LDA
1234   98765432

ACKNOWLEDGMENTS

Almost all the photographs in this book are by Rosemary Low and depict
birds at the Loro Parque zoological park in Tenerife, of which she is the
Curator. The Author wishes to acknowledge the help of Sandra Mason
and Inmaculada Mendez at Loro Parque, without whose patience in
holding the chicks, photographs of young birds would have been
impossible.
    Other photographs inside the book are by courtesy of Ardea
London/Graham Chapman (page 68), Dennis Avon (88, 106), *Cage and
Aviary Birds* magazine (48, 70, 131) and Robin Williams (66).

CONTENTS

Foreword 6
Introduction 7
Features of a parrot 8
Accident prevention 9
Amazon Parrots 10
Antibiotics 11
Aratinga conures 12
Aviary 13
Barnardius parakeets 15
Beak 16
Biting 17
Black Cockatoos 17
Amazons 18–19
Blindness 21
Bolborhynchus parakeets 21
Conures (1) 22–3
Breeding 25
Brooders 25
Conures (2) 26–7
Buying 28
Cages 29
Cockatoos (1) 30–31
Caiques 33
Chalcopsitta lories 34
Charmosyna lories 35
Chicks 36
Chicks, failure to feed 36
CITES 37
Clutch 37
Cockatiel 38
Cockatoos 39
Conservation 41
Conure 41
Crimson-winged Parakeets 42
Diet 43
Eclectus Parrots 44
Eggs 45
Enicognathus conures 45
Eos lories 47
Eunymphicus parakeets 47
Exhibiting 48
Feather 49
Cockatoos (2) 50–51
Feather plucking 52
Feral parrots 52
Fig Parrots 53
Cockatoos (3) 54–5
Foot 56
Force-feeding 56
Fractures 57
Lories (1) 58–9
French molt 60
Fruits 60
Lories (2) 62
Lorikeets 63
Gang Gang Cockatoo 64
Geoffroyus parrots 64

Glossopsitta lorikeets 65
Grass parakeets 65
Gray Parrot 66
Grit 67
Ground Parrot 68
Guaiabero 69
Habitat 69
Handling 70
Hand-rearing 71
Hanging Parrots 71
Hatching failure 73
Hawk-headed Parrot 74
Hyacinthine Macaw 75
Hygiene 76
Illness 76
Incubation 76
Incubators 77
Infrared lamp 78
Kaka 79
Kakapo 79
Kakarikis 79
Kea 80
King Parakeets 80
Parakeets (1) 82–3
Leptosittaca conure 84
Lories 84
Lorius lories 85
Lovebirds 85
Parakeets (2) 86–7
Macaws 89
Parakeets (3) 90–91
Molting 93
Macaws 94–5
Nandayus conure 96
Nannopsittaca parrotlets 96
Nectar 97
Neopsittacus lories 97
Nest boxes 98
Nest sites in the wild 100
Net 101
Night Parrot 101
Ognorhynchus parrot 102
Oreopsittacus lorikeet 102
Parrotlets (*Forpus*) 103
Patagonian Conure 103
Pesquet's Parrot 104
Phigys lory 105
Pileated Parakeet 105
Pionopsitta parrots 106
Pionus parrots 106
Poicephalus parrots 107
Polytelis parakeets 109

Protein, animal 110
Psephotus parakeets 110
Pseudeos lory 111
Psittacella parrots 112
Psittacine beak and feather disease syndrome 112
Psittacula parakeets 113
Rosellas 114
Vasas 115
Psittinus parrot 116
Purple-bellied Parrot 116
Pygmy Parrots 117
Pyrrhura conures 117
A miscellany of parrots (1) 118–19
Quaker Parakeet 120
Racket-tailed parrots 121
Red mites 121
A miscellany of parrots (2) 122–3
Rhynchopsitta parrots 124
Ringing (banding) 125
A miscellany of parrots (3) 126–7
Rodent control 128
Rosellas 129
Security 130
Seed 130
Seed, sunflower 130
Selling 131
Sexing, feather chromosome 132
Sexing, surgical 132
Sexual dimorphism 133
Shining Parrots 134
Short-tailed Parrot 135
Spix's Macaw 135
Spraying 135
Stress 136
Swift Parakeet 137
Tanygnathus parrots 137
Teaching parrots to talk 138
Touit parrotlets 138
Trichoglossus lorikeets 139
Vasa parrots 140
Vegetables 140
Veterinary advice 141
Vini lories 141
Water 142
Winter care 142
Worming 143
Zoonosis 144

FOREWORD

Ernest Hemingway's pet parrot still sits on a perch in a bar in Barcelona – old, wise, enigmatic and given to uttering an occasional salty epithet; the epitome of this unique and intriguing family of birds.

Parrots are different from other birds, not just in any physical respect or by dint of their high intelligence, but in their attitude to *Homo sapiens*. These birds that can, as Shakespeare put it, "laugh at a bagpiper", seem to me shrewd observers of the human condition, creatures whose approbation and friendship have to be painstakingly won. Parrots don't curry favor like lap-dogs.

Nowadays, with many psittacine species greatly endangered by environmental hazards and illegal and unscrupulous catching, there is a welcome boom in interest in and concern for parrots worldwide. Their value in financial terms soars, no bad thing for the birds themselves if it makes humans treasure them more, and there are new and fruitful developments in captive reproduction and rearing of an expanding range of species. In my own field of exotic animal medicine, specialist veterinarians with particular interest and skills in psittacine diseases and surgery are contributing more and more to better health for these animals.

But still there exists a great need for more information and assistance to be made available to both the *aficionados* and the devoted pet parrot owners. So often I come across well-meaning and doting parrot fanciers who know virtually nothing about the magnificent creatures that they possess. Birds are still bought from dealers who give little or no, or sometimes erroneous, advice as to their proper maintenance.

Now at last, a comprehensive, clearly laid out guide to things parrot is at hand. Rosemary Low is an internationally acknowledged expert on these creatures and her instructions on everything to do with parrots, together with fascinating information on the wild and gorgeously-colored world of the family Psittacidae, including the rarest and least-known species, are masterly.

Even the most inexperienced owner of a foul-mouthed African Gray with a penchant for chocolate drops and an aversion to anything in trousers, can now reach for the "bible" and dip into it with confidence, profit and much pleasure.

DAVID C. TAYLOR BVMS, FRCVS, FZS
KEIGHLEY, YORKSHIRE

INTRODUCTION

Parrots are many things to many people. They may be cherished and adored pets (in sensitive care), irreplaceable companions (to the lonely, aged or housebound), perhaps even an unwanted nuisance (in the wrong hands), or an absorbing hobby (to the breeder with a few aviaries). They may be the means of earning a living (to dealers and importers, professional breeders and even trainers) or, to the uninitiated, "the birds that talk" in the local zoo. To me they are a way of life.

A never ending source of joy and satisfaction, they are also the cause of frequent disappointment and heartbreak, as is inevitable with all livestock. Involved with parrots before I left school, it was not long until they took over my professional life, too, first as deputy editor of the weekly magazine *Cage and Aviary Birds*, then as a freelance writer and author on psittacines, and now as curator of the world's most comprehensive collection of parrots, Loro Parque in Tenerife.

There is so much to learn about these fascinating birds that a lifetime of study can reveal only the tip of the iceberg. I am privileged to work with over 200 species and every day with them throws more light on their behavior, their needs, their beauty and their personalities.

The beginner has a whole new world of discovery ahead and a thousand and one questions. Many of these can be answered only as the result of personal experience: others, I hope, will be found in the pages which follow. But there will be many unanswered questions because no two parrots are precisely alike: what suits one is not good for another. So observe your birds very carefully and spend much time with them. Only in this way will you develop the rapport which is essential for success.

ROSEMARY LOW
LORO PARQUE, TENERIFE

Features of a parrot

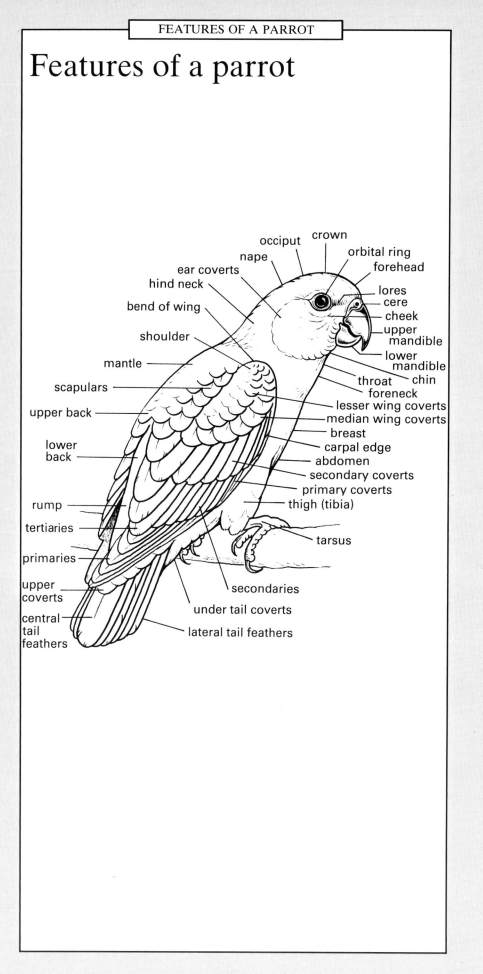

occiput · crown · nape · orbital ring · forehead · ear coverts · lores · cere · hind neck · cheek · bend of wing · upper mandible · shoulder · lower mandible · mantle · throat · chin · scapulars · foreneck · lesser wing coverts · upper back · median wing coverts · breast · lower back · carpal edge · abdomen · secondary coverts · primary coverts · thigh (tibia) · rump · tertiaries · tarsus · primaries · secondaries · upper coverts · under tail coverts · central tail feathers · lateral tail feathers

A

ACCIDENT PREVENTION

One of the joys of pet-bird ownership is allowing a bird to share one's room or house, rather than cofining it to a cage. Unfortunately, however, many accidents can befall a bird that has such freedom. Birds are highly inquisitive and, like young children, should not be left unattended.

Risk of accident can be reduced by the following precautions before letting a bird out of its cage:

1 Close all doors and windows. Place a guard across an open fireplace.
2 If the windows are not protected by net curtains, close the draperies on the first few occasions on which a bird is let out of its cage, to prevent it

Before allowing your parrot its freedom within the house, remove all potential hazards and close doors and windows.

flying into the window. The bird's neck could be broken by a headlong collision.
3 Do not allow birds their freedom in the kitchen – a highly hazardous place. They could inhale toxic fumes, fall into containers of water or fat, or land on a hot stove. Remember that an electric hot plate retains heat for a long time after being switched off. One of the most frequent accidents results when cookware, coated with Teflon or some other nonstick material, is heated while empty.

If this coating is allowed to burn, resulting fumes are lethal to birds. They die in minutes. Fumes from self-cleaning ovens are also dangerous.
4 Birds, more than humans, are sensitive to fumes; canaries were therefore formerly used to detect gas in coal mines. Do not use aerosols in a room occupied by a bird. Insect sprays are also dangerous. Keep a dog or cat out of doors for a couple of hours after it has been sprayed for fleas. Remove all birds from the house if a room has to be fumigated.
5 Do not allow a bird its freedom in a room where an electric fan is operating.
6 If birds have access to a bathroom, keep the lavatory seat lid down. Cover any other water container, such as an aquarium.
7 Remove or replace lead items, such as lead curtain weights. Do not use lead paint in areas to which birds have access. Lead is highly toxic.
8 Remove pot plants and cacti; some are poisonous, and others could be damaged by the bird.
9 Do not leave matches where birds will have access to them. They, too, are toxic.
10 Certain felt-tipped marker pens are extremely toxic. Pens and pencils should also be removed from reach.
11 A parrot could be killed, or badly shocked, if it bit through the wire to an attached electrical appliance. Make sure these are not exposed.
12 Cats, dogs, and other household pets are a great source of danger to the smaller parrots, while large parrots can themselves prove dangerous to small pets.

Other household pets can be a source of danger to parrots.

A Double
Yellow-headed
Amazon (*Amazona
ochrocephala
oratrix*), aged 16
days.

Agapornis – see *LOVEBIRDS*

Alisterus – see *KING
PARAKEETS*

AMAZON PARROTS (*Amazona*)
Amazons form one of the largest,
most distinctive, and well-known
groups of parrots. There are about
26 species (opinions vary as to
whether some should be considered
species or subspecies). Amazons
originate from South and Central
America, and also the Caribbean
Islands.

In size they range from about 24
cm (9½ in) in the smallest
subspecies of the Spectacled
Amazon (*A. albifrons nana*) and
the closely related Yellow-lored
Amazon (*A. xantholora*) to about
46 cm (18 in) in the magnificent
and greatly endangered Imperial
Amazon (*A. imperialis*).

All but one species of Amazon
are basically green with contrasting
markings on the head and tail (and
also on the wings, but this is
evident in most species only when
the birds are in flight). Recognition
can be made mainly by head
coloration which varies from
unremarkable to extremely
beautiful. Pronounced sexual
dimorphism is confined to one
species, *xantholora*. (See *SEXUAL
DIMORPHISM*.) The body shape
does vary but most Amazons are
compact and solid in appearance
and the beak and feet are strong.
The tail is fairly short and square.

Personality varies greatly from
species to species and also among
individuals. Some, such as the
Yellow-fronted Amazon (also
called Yellow-crowned), the
Double Yellow-headed and the
Yellow-naped (all subspecies of
ochrocephala), and the Festive
Amazon (*A. festiva*) are wonderful

mimics; they can copy human
speech, laugh, and sing.

Many Amazons have wonderful
qualities as pets, but most have the
disadvantage of indulging in
regular periods of screaming
(morning and evening). This fact
must be borne in mind because it is
serious enough to disturb other
occupants of the house, as well as
neighbors. At their best, however,
Amazons are affectionate, playful
and amusing.

Many pet birds are devoted to
one person, or will tolerate
attention from men or from
women, but not both. My own pet
of 25 years is a Yellow-fronted
Amazon – a female who dispels the
myth that parrots prefer humans of
the opposite sex to themselves. She
does not tolerate men (or other
Amazons!). Amazons can bite
hard, if excited or teased, and are
not recommended as children's
pets.

As aviary birds Amazons are
extremely rewarding, providing
they are tame. Most wild-caught
adults will also become less
nervous in time. Fortunately, with
every year that passes, the
proportion of aviary-bred to
wild-caught birds increases.

Individual preferences in diet are
very noticeable in this group, and
thus a wide variety should be
offered. The basic diet can consist
of a mixture of soaked or sprouted
sunflower and/or safflower seeds,
boiled maize, sprouted mung
beans, and boiled peanut kernels
mixed in one container. Another
container can be used for dry
seeds: approximately equal parts of
sunflower or safflower, canary,
oats, buckwheat, pine nuts, and a
little hemp in winter. Many
Amazons also relish a millet spray.
A third container should be

provided for fruits and vegetables.

A very wide variety of table scraps is enjoyed by Amazons: cooked vegetables, lean meat, bread, toast, cake, pasta, rice, yogurt, cheese, and the occasional potato chip as a treat. In moderation these are excellent. Pet Amazons greatly look forward to meal times!

Just prior to the breeding season, and until the end of this period, bread and milk, or a whole-wheat bread mixture can be given. The latter is used by many successful breeders. To the whole-wheat bread mixture is added a little raw egg, grated carrot, and endive, for example. This is then baked.

Amazons are not the easiest parrots to induce to breed in captivity. Many pairs are infertile, or make no attempt to nest: the latter should be moved to a new location or given new partners. Infertility often stems from the fact that the male and female have not come into breeding condition at the same time.

Amazons usually lay only one clutch per year, although some females can be induced to lay a second clutch if the eggs are removed for artificial incubation. Generally, the smaller and medium-sized Amazons, such as the Cuban (*A. leucocephala leucocephala*), Blue-fronted (*A. aestiva aestiva*) and Yellow-fronted (*A. ochrocephala*), are easier to breed than the large species.

Sex can be determined surgically or by feather follicle sexing. (See SEXING, FEATHER CHROMOSOME.) It is impossible to sex them by sight, and even those very familiar with Amazon behavior may guess wrong.

Amazons lay two to four eggs (only rarely one or five), which the female incubates for 25 to 28 days. In most countries, April or May is the usual time of egg laying by captive birds, but eggs are occasionally laid as early as February or March. The young spend eight or nine weeks in the nest. Immature plumage is generally, although not always, duller than that of the adults.

A sure indication of immaturity is eye color. In the majority of adult Amazons, the iris of the eye is orange (in a few species, e.g., the rare Jamaican Black-billed Amazon [*A. agilis*] it is dark brown). In all young birds, however, it is grayish-brown, changing to dull orange (where applicable) by the age of about five months. An Amazon for a pet should be obtained before the immature eye color changes. This is the only guarantee that the bird is very young.

Amazons do very well in suspended outdoor aviaries in localities that do not normally experience temperatures below freezing in winter. The minimum recommended length is 2.7 m (9 ft). Traditional-type aviaries are also suitable.

Anodorhynchus MACAWS – see under *HYACINTHINE MACAW*

ANTIBIOTICS
Antibiotics are an important resource of veterinary medicine.

Fresh greens such as sowthistle, are an important part of the diet of most Amazons. Seen here are two Mealy Amazons (*Amazona farinosa farinosa*).

They should be used only as prescribed by an avian veterinarian and never as a precautionary measure. Birds that regularly receive antibiotics will become resistant to them.

The same is true of antifungal preparations. Some breeders give hand-reared chicks Nystatin (a fungicide) to prevent their getting candidiasis. By doing this, however, they disturb the balance of the intestinal flora.

A competent veterinarian will obtain a fecal sample from the bird to be treated. From this he or she will prepare an antibiogram; that is, the fecal sample will be cultured on a plate, using several different types of antibiotics, to discover which antibiotic should be the most effective. Valuable time can be wasted when a broad-spectrum antibiotic is given in the hope that it will cure the problem.

After a few days it may be necessary to change to a different antibiotic if the first has not proved effective. With sick birds time is precious; all too often a bird's life is lost because the wrong treatment has been prescribed. Antibiotics inhibit the growth of bacteria, but are not effective against viruses. To ensure correct dosage a veterinarian needs to know the approximate weight of a bird that is to be given antibiotics.

***Aprosmictus* PARAKEETS** – see *CRIMSON-WINGED PARAKEETS*

***Ara* MACAWS** – see *MACAWS (Ara)*

***Aratinga* CONURES**
These Conures originate from Mexico, Central America, and from all the tropical regions of South America. The size range of the species is between 23 cm (9 in) and 36 cm (14 in).

This is not an easy group for the uninitiated to recognize, as there is great variation in size, and, although most members of the genus are mainly green, there are some dramatic exceptions. The long tapered tail is common to all members of the genus, however.

This genus could be divided into three groups:
1 The minority – Sun, Jendaya, and Queen of Bavaria's (Golden) Conures, which are brilliantly colored. The Queen of Bavaria's Conure is uncharacteristically large, with a very large beak. All golden yellow, its coloration is unforgettable. An exceptionally intelligent and interesting bird, its drawbacks are its high price and its very loud, harsh voice.
2 Another group is basically green, with red markings on the head and/or scattered red feathers in the region of the head and neck. Given the similarity of some species in immature plumage to other species, identification of this group can be difficult. For example, the Mitred (*A. mitrata*) and Red-masked (*A. erythrogenys*) Conures are easily distinguished in adult plumage and also in the first immature plumage.

On leaving the nest, Mitred Conures are duller red on the head than adults and also have less red, whereas young Red-masked have only a narrow band of brownish-red on the forehead. At about six months old, however, both species have similar scattered red feathers on the head. They can best be distinguished by the larger size of *mitrata* and by the color of the skin surrounding the eye, which is yellowish in *erythrogenys* (deeper yellow in adults) and white in *mitrata*.
3 The remaining members of the genus are mainly green with dull or contrasting colors, such as orange or blue, on the head.
Behaviorally, all birds of this genus are very much alike, except perhaps that of the Queen of Bavaria's Conure, which seems different but in fact its actions are merely exaggerated. They will all threaten a possible enemy by swaying, ruffling the feathers of the head, and shrieking loudly. All have unpleasant voices, thereby disqualifying themselves from many aviaries.

The diet should consist of a mixture of small seeds, such as canary, white millet, oats or groats, buckwheat, a little hemp, and small sunflower seeds. Conures can also be offered a mixture of soaked or sprouted sunflower seeds, sprouted mung beans, boiled peanut kernels, chopped apple, orange, carrot, and spinach. Most fruits, such as grapes and pears, will be relished.

Many species of *Aratinga*, especially those in the first and second groups, breed very readily in captivity. They are excellent parents and will also foster the young of other species. They generally lay three or four eggs, which are incubated by the female for about 25 days.

On hatching, chicks are fairly well covered in white down (yellow in Sun Conures). They have a loud food-soliciting cry that is something like that of Amazon parrots. The young spend about eight weeks in the nest, venturing out for short periods only at first, and always returning to the nest to sleep.

The Sun Conure is considered the most beautiful of the smaller members of the genus and is perhaps the most sought after. The vivid yellow and orange of its plumage ensures a demand for the young. The price is thus quite high, although not out of reach for most breeders. The Queen of Bavaria's Conure is considerably more expensive.

Many species of *Aratinga* will breed in suspended aviaries, traditional aviaries, or large cages. Plumage is alike in male and female, and thus surgical or chromosome sexing is recommended. Members of the genus usually commence to breed at two years old. Some species are single-brooded (having only one brood a season), others are double-brooded. Hardy and easy to feed, they can be recommended for beginners.

AVIARY

This term is applied to a large cage used for keeping birds, generally out of doors. The most usual design has a solid floor, a framework of timber (metal for very destructive species), the sides and roof of welded mesh (also called hardware cloth), and a sheltered or totally enclosed area for roosting.

The following aspects should be taken into consideration before building an aviary:

1 Building permission – is this required from any local planning authority?
2 The site – this should be sheltered and preferably in view of the house, but, for security reasons, not too evident to passersby. (Thefts of parrots are common and a constant source of worry to keepers of these attractive birds.) The aviary should not be where it will disturb neighbors. It should be on flat land not liable to flooding. Allow for expansion; more aviaries are likely to follow and servicing them is much easier in a compact area.
3 The type of structure – there are many possible designs and layouts. If you can, visit a few parrot breeders before starting to build, to ask for ideas and advice. Ask breeders how their ideal setup would differ from that currently in use; you can thus profit from their mistakes! Altering aviaries is expensive, usually impracticable, and often impossible.
4 The setting – a single aviary or

Planting with shrubs and vines can enhance the appearance of garden aviaries.

A neatly built structure, such as this range of aviaries for macaws, will be the focal point of any garden.

range of aviaries can be attractively incorporated into a garden. Set amid trees, surrounded by flowers, and covered in nonpoisonous flowering vines, such as honeysuckle, Virginia creeper, or clematis, the aviary becomes the center of interest in the garden.

5 Before beginning to build, carefully consider the importance of making the aviary floor vermin-proof. Rats, mice, and other rodents are a health hazard and a threat to the lives of aviary occupants; they also consume enormous amounts of food. No matter how well a conventional aviary is constructed, or how small the wire mesh, the enclosure will not be vermin-proof unless the floor is made of concrete, or 9-mm (⅜-in) welded mesh is buried under the ground. Concrete is a hygienic material, provided that it is regularly hosed or scrubbed. A concrete floor should be constructed so that it slopes slightly towards a drainage channel.

Alternatively (and I prefer this for lories), large stones make an excellent base, regular hosing being all that is required to keep it clean.

It should be noted that soil floors are highly unsatisfactory. They are impossible to clean thoroughly and can be sterilized only with a blowtorch. They are not recommended.

6 The construction – tubular steel is recommended for the framework. Initially it is a little more expensive than wood, but there is no maintenance. Unlike wood, steel will last a lifetime. It cannot be destroyed, or its appearance spoiled by the occupants. Various shaped joints can be purchased and joined together using a plumber's pipe wrench. Wire can be pop-riveted, soldered, or welded to the framework.

7 The shelter – this can be open-fronted or totally enclosed, according to the climate and location. In the northern states, a fully enclosed shelter is recommended. The birds can be kept inside in inclement weather and lighting and heating can be employed if necessary. (See *INFRA-RED LAMP*.) The shelter must be light, with a window in the side or roof, or birds will refuse to enter.

Covering a glass window with welded mesh is essential to prevent escapes in the event of breakage. Glass with inlaid welded mesh can be used if the price is not prohibitive. Locate the entrance to the shelter so that roosting birds are not in a draft. Cover the roof with roofing felt to ensure that it is waterproof. To create an attractive appearance on a sloping roof, roofing shingles can be used.

The roof of the flight area must be covered for part of its length, preferably over the highest perch – the preferred roosting location of birds that do not sleep in their nest boxes. The entire roof can be made of welded mesh, the additional cover being placed above this.

8 The door – situate this where

B

there is least risk of escape. In a single aviary, a safety porch (double doors, one being closed before the next is opened) is advisable. In a range of aviaries, a service passage situated along the back of the shelters is strongly recommended. The roof of the passage can be covered.

If the door into the aviary opens into the service passage, there is no possibility of escape. Every aviary must have its own access door. Entrance via another aviary not only causes disturbance, but is a hazard: should a door be left open, another bird may enter, with fatal results. Many parrots will instantly kill any other bird that enters their territory.

9 The feeding hatch – this eliminates the need to enter the aviary at feeding time, thus reducing disturbance to the occupants (especially important when they are breeding). The hatch also reduces the risk of escape and is essential in aviaries lacking a safety porch. The hatch should be just large enough to admit the food and water containers. These can be hooked onto the welded mesh near the hatch, or placed on a shelf below it. The hatch should be hinged at the top, so that if it is left unfastened, it automatically drops down. Alternatively, it can be constructed on a revolving principle, i.e., the actual shelf rotates, to reveal the containers that are slotted into the shelf or clipped into special holders. In this case, a wire guard on one end of the shelf, or a strip of welded mesh surrounding it, and at the same height as the hatch, will prevent escapes.

A feeding hatch is recommended, both to save time and prevent disturbing the aviary occupants.

Barnardius PARAKEETS

These large broadtailed parakeets, which range in size from 33–38 cm (13–15 in), including the long tail, are mainly green, with a yellow collar and contrasting areas of blue and yellow, and also red or black in some subspecies. They originate in Australia.

These birds are unsuitable as pets, in both behavior and temperament. They are at their best in a long aviary, because they need a lot of exercise. Suspended cages are not recommended, because their tails soon become damaged in this type of accommodation. They do best in enclosures which are at least 4.5 m (15 ft) long and 2.1 m (7 ft) high.

Among the more highly priced, and usually less free-breeding Australian parakeets, members of this genus are not considered suitable for beginners.

A most attractive feature of these birds is the way they waggle their broad tails from side to side when excited, even in flight. Their plumage, of various shades of green and yellow, generally lacks sharply contrasting colors, except for the Port Lincoln Parakeet, which has a black head.

Sexual dimorphism is either not very marked or does not exist. (See *SEXUAL DIMORPHISM*.)

There are two species. Barnard's Parakeet (*B. barnardi barnardi*) is bright green with a dark red frontal band, light blue on the cheeks, shoulders, and wing margins, dark blue on the mantle and the tip of the tail, with a yellow nuchal collar and yellow on the lower breast. Young birds have a brownish crown and nape and a grayish-green back and mantle.

A most attractive subspecies, which closely resembles the Mallee Ringneck or Barnard's Parakeet, is the softly marked Cloncurry Parakeet (*B. b. macgillivrayi*). Mainly pale green, it has part of the cheeks blue and the nuchal collar and abdomen yellow. Young birds have a dull red frontal band, which disappears in two to three months.

The Port Lincoln Parakeet (*B. zonarius zonarius*) is a very handsome bird. It has part of its cheeks blue, but the head is otherwise black, or more brownish-black in some females. The abdomen and also the nuchal collar are yellow. Plumage is otherwise mainly dark green.

The Twenty-eight Parakeet (*B. z. semitorquatus*) receives its unusual name from its call, which is said to resemble this number. Its plumage differs from that of the Port Lincoln Parakeet in that the abdomen is green, not yellow.

These birds should be offered as much green food as possible, both before the breeding season, to stimulate them to nest, and during the rearing period. They extract juices from the stems and eat the leaves. Carrot, apple, corn on the cob, and other fruits and vegetables should be offered, as well as a good variety of seeds, such as canary, oats or groats, hemp, buckwheat, white millet, sunflower, and safflower. These parakeets are very fond of hawthorn berries.

Members of this genus lay four to six eggs, and occasionally as many as seven. These are incubated by the female for nineteen days. These birds are generally single-brooded, but can prove prolific in a more favorable climate than that of Britain, for example.

BEAK
This is one of the distinctive features by which members of the parrot family are recognized.

In parrots, the upper and lower mandible is hinged to the skull, giving separate vertical movement. The upper surface of the beak is renewed, a little at a time, in an irregular shedding process. The beak actually consists of layers of cells, renewed by proliferation from the basal layer as the outer layers die and become keratinized. Above the upper mandible is a soft, thickened area, known as the cere. In some parrots, such as Eclectus, this is feathered.

In some species there is sexual dimorphism of the beak color and shape. In *Psittacula* Parakeets, Eclectus Parrots, and one subspecies of a *Bolborhynchus* Parakeet, males and females have different bill coloration. In Keas,

the beak is longer and more curved in the male. See *SEXUAL DIMORPHISM*.)

Chicks within the egg develop an egg tooth, near the tip of the upper mandible, with which to pierce the shell when they hatch. The myth that this is shed after a few days is perpetuated in almost every book on birds! In fact, as the chick and its bill grow, the egg tooth forms part of the beak. The egg tooth can still be observed in some chicks as old as three weeks.

There are a variety of beak shapes in different species, the shape being adapted to feeding habits. One of the best adapted is that of the Red-capped Parrot (*Purpureicephalus spurius*), known as the Pileated Parakeet outside Australia. It feeds mainly on seeds, especially those of the Australian gum tree (*Eucalyptus calophylla*). The narrow, elongated upper mandible, and the gap between the two mandibles, appear to be an adaptation for feeding on the eucalyptus seeds, which are enclosed in a bowl-shaped pod with a rim. The bowl is impenetrable; the seeds can be reached only through the top of the pod.

The parrot with the narrowest, most elongated bill is the Slender-billed Conure (*Enicognathus leptorhynchus*) from Chile. (Its beak shape is not unlike that of the Slender-billed Cockatoo, which is a ground-feeding bird.) This conure is equally adept at extracting pips

A year after breaking off nearly half of its upper mandible in an accident, the beak of this Maximilian's Parrot (*Pionus maximiliani maximiliani*) had grown back almost to the normal length.

from apples or at digging in the ground – yet the reason for its unusual bill shape is not known.

The size of the beak is also related to feeding habits. The largest beak of any parrot (also the largest in relation to body size) is that of the Hyacinthine Macaw (*Anodorhynchus hyacinthinus*); the beak's enormous strength enables it to open any nut. Brazil nuts are opened as easily as a Gray Parrot would extract a peanut from its shell.

Many captive parrots suffer accidents to the beak, usually to the upper mandible, which may be ripped or broken off in its entirety. If this happens, the mandible will never grow again, and, except for a lory (which can survive on a liquid diet), there is little chance that the bird will survive. However, if even a small part of the mandible remains, it will grow again. This will take months, possibly over a year in severe cases, but provided that the bird survives the initial shock, it will live and can learn to eat soft items of food.

In some parrots, growth of the beak may be abnormally rapid, or perhaps irregular as the result of an injury. In such cases regular trimming is necessary. This is best done by a veterinarian who has the proper tools, such as an electric drill or file. A sharp pair of nail clippers can be used for small birds. Overgrowth of the beak may simply be due to lack of wood (preferably fresh branches) for gnawing. Some species, such as Fig Parrots, will quickly acquire overgrown beaks if wood is not provided.

BITING
There are three basic reasons why a parrot bites: out of fear, excitement or sheer high spirits, and out of malice. The latter is impossible to cure. Birds that bite for no reason other than because they enjoy doing so, are best used for breeding rather than pets. Most parrots, even tame ones, will bite out of fear – when caught, for example, and held in the hand. Many parrots that are tame enough to climb all over their owners, will bite if hands are closed around their bodies, or if certain parts of their bodies are touched.

Some hand-reared parrots, macaws and Grays, for example,

go through a stage, at about six months old, when they become very boisterous and excitable and start to nip. From the outset, they should be tapped lightly on the beak and the command "No!" given. They can thus be made to understand that such behavior is not acceptable.

Tame birds may also bite out of jealousy, for example when another parrot is placed too close to the bird while it is perched on its owner. The tame one cannot bite the intruder, so it bites its owner instead. A tame bird may also bite out of frustration or temper, for example on being returned to its cage when it does not wish to go.

BLACK COCKATOOS
The Black Cockatoos are very large parrots, totally distinct from other cockatoos because their plumage is almost entirely black. There are two genera: *Calyptorhynchus* (three species) and *Probisciger* (one species).

Calyptorhynchus originates from Australia. These are extremely beautiful and highly intelligent birds. Sexual dimorphism is obvious or only slight. They range in size from 50–65 cm (20–26 in). They are rare in captivity.

The diet in captivity should be mainly seeds and nuts, such as sunflower, canary grass seeds, peanuts, pine nuts, walnuts, and Brazil nuts. The White-tailed Black Cockatoo needs more greens than the other species.

Although rare in captivity, the Banksian or Red-tailed Black Cockatoo (*C. magnificus*) is the best-known member of the genus. The male is all black, except for a broad band of scarlet on the tail feathers, except the central pair. The tail is barred with red and black in the female, whose head and shoulders are marked with yellow spots.

Its length is 60 cm (23 in). Most immature birds resemble the female, but some young males leave the nest in adult plumage. This is normally acquired at two years and nine months.

This cockatoo occurs in eastern, northern and southwestern Australia, being more common in the north. It usually nests in eucalyptus trees. One egg is laid, but occasionally two. Incubation is carried out by the female for 28

Amazons

Vinaceous Amazon *(Amazona vinacea)* – another Brazilian species threatened by loss of habitat.

Above: Finsch's Amazon *(Amazona finschi)* used to be freely available, but the export of Mexican parrots is no longer permitted.

Pretre's Amazon *(Amazona pretrei)* – a rare species from Brazil.

Lilacine Amazon *(Amazona autumnalis lilacina)* from Ecuador – rare in captivity and declining in the wild.

Blue-fronted Amazons *(Amazona aestiva xanthopteryx)*, which are imported today, originate from Paraguay and Argentina.

days. The young spend 12 to 13 weeks in the nest. In the wild they stay with their parents until the parents nest again during the following year.

The nature of this species is exceptionally gentle and affectionate. They seldom use their large beaks in defense. Hand-reared birds, especially males, crave human attention. This can be a problem, in that they can become imprinted on people and are then useless for breeding purposes. They should be introduced to their own species as soon as they are independent. They are nervous and sensitive at this stage, and the introduction must be made with extreme care.

The glossy Black Cockatoo (*C. lathami*) is distinguished from the Banksian Cockatoo by its brownish head coloration and smaller size. Some birds have irregular orange-yellow markings on the head and neck. The female has the red tail band, barred with black and speckled with yellow: there are no yellow spots on the body, except some mottling about the head and neck.

In length it is about 50 cm (19–20 in). Immature birds cannot be sexed: they are all spotted and barred, but by one and a half years some males have lost these markings on ear and wing coverts.

This species is found in eastern Australia (central Queensland to eastern Victoria). It feeds almost entirely on the seeds of the casuarina tree. Its nest is a hollow branch or the trunk of a tree. Only the female incubates the single egg – for about 32 days.

Until fairly recently it was believed that maintaining this species in captivity was dependent upon a supply of casuarina seeds, but this is not so. Australian breeders feed these birds mainly on sunflower seeds, of which they should have an unlimited supply. The Glossy Cockatoo has never been kept in captivity outside Australia. Like the Banksian Cockatoo, its personality is friendly and affectionate.

There are two subspecies of Black Cockatoo (*C. funereus*): the Funereal or Yellow-tailed Cockatoo (*C. f. funereus*) and the White-tailed or Baudin's Cockatoo (*C. f. baudinii*). The Funereal Cockatoo is brownish-black, the

feathers margined with yellow. The undersides of the tail feathers are yellow, freckled with brownish-black (more prominently in the female). Her ear coverts are also a brighter yellow. In the White-tailed Cockatoo, the male's ear coverts are grayish, otherwise the areas of plumage that are yellow on the Funereal Cockatoo are white. In both subspecies, the bill is dark gray in the male and horn-colored in the female.

A woodland bird, found in small groups, the Funereal Cockatoo occurs in eastern and southeastern Australia, and also Tasmania, King Island and the larger Bass Strait islands; and the White-tailed Cockatoo occurs in the southwestern corner of Western Australia. Sadly, it is endangered by habitat destruction. Breeding information is similar to that given for the Banksian Cockatoo.

There are few *C. funereus* in captivity, especially outside Australia. Their personality is aloof – totally different from that of the other two members of the genus.

A White-tailed Black Cockatoo (*Calyptorhynchus funereus baudinii*).

The Palm Cockatoo (*Probosciger aterrimus*) originates from New Guinea and the top of Cape York Peninsula in north Queensland (Australia). The female is usually smaller than the male, with a shorter upper mandible, but the size of this bird varies between about 70 and 80 cm (27–32 in) according to locality of origin. It is rare in captivity.

It has an entirely gray-black plumage, very long, narrow crest feathers, and a large area of bare red facial skin (pale pink in birds in poor condition). The tongue is unusual, red, tipped with black. In immature birds, the feathers of the underparts and the under wing coverts are margined with pale yellow. On leaving the nest, young birds' beaks are edged with white and the skin surrounding their eyes is white.

Its diet in captivity should be similar to *Calyptorhynchus*, plus almonds, for which Palm Cockatoos have a great liking. Some Palm Cockatoos will eat fruit, such as banana, apple, and pear.

Captive breeding has been achieved in a few collections in Europe and Australia.

This species builds a platform of splintered twigs inside its nest (to protect eggs or young from excessive rainfall). The single egg is incubated by both male and female, or by the female only, for about 34 days. The young bird spends about 12 weeks in the nest.

This is another gentle species. Wild-caught birds tend to be very shy. The trade in wild birds of the species is not likely to continue, and thus captive breeding is of the greatest importance.

BLINDNESS
Blindness in parrots can result from injury, infection, poisoning and, especially in aged birds, cataracts. When affected by the latter, there may be partial vision. A blind bird may have an eye missing or one eye that looks glazed or opaque. Sometimes only its behavior indicates that it is blind, but one can easily test for vision by moving one's hand towards the suspected blind eye.

When a bird becomes totally blind, the decision may have to be made whether or not to end its life. This must depend entirely on individual circumstances. Some birds may be hardly inconvienced by blindness, incredible as this may seem. At Loro Parque there is a totally blind female Yellow-bibbed Lory (*Lorius chlorocercus*), a species from the Solomon Islands, which is very rare in captivity. She is an extremely valuable breeding bird. To watch her moving about the aviary it is hard to believe that she is blind until she descends to the ground and begins to use her beak to feel for the sides of the aviary.

The quality of this bird's life is hardly impaired by her blindness, but in other cases, such as where this condition is associated with senile debility, it would be kinder to have a blind bird put to sleep. There is, however, no cause to end the life of a tame pet bird which has become blind if it can still enjoy its food and the attentions of its owner and, indeed, still be a source of pleasure.

BLUE-RUMPED PARROT – see *Psittinus*

Bolborhynchus PARAKEETS
These parakeets originate in Central America and the western part of South America.

The smallest of the neotropical parakeets, the diminutiveness of these birds lends them a special charm. Although their plumage is quite different, members of the public often mistake them for budgerigars because most species of *Bolborhynchus* are similar to these little birds in size and shape. The tail varies, however, from long and tapered to short.

Only the Lineolated Parakeet is well established in captivity – and only in a few European countries. Most newly imported birds are difficult to establish, those from high altitudes (especially the Aymara) being extremely difficult. The death rate is so high that the capture and export of wild-caught birds should be discouraged. Caring aviculturists should buy only captive-bred birds, and there are few of these. Unless more breeders concentrate on these totally delightful little birds, they will be lost to aviculture. This would be regrettable, because their quiet voices and small size make them ideal for apartment dwellers.

The diet for *Bolborhynchus*

TOP: The White-eyed Conure (*Aratinga leucophthalmus*) is found over most of tropical South America.
BOTTOM: An Hispaniolan Conure (*Aratinga chloroptera*) from Santo Domingo and Haiti.

Conures (1)

The Lesser Patagonian Conure *(Cyanoliseus patagonus patagonus)* is the only subspecies that is common in captivity.

The Blue-throated Conure *(Pyrrhura cruentata)* from Brazil.

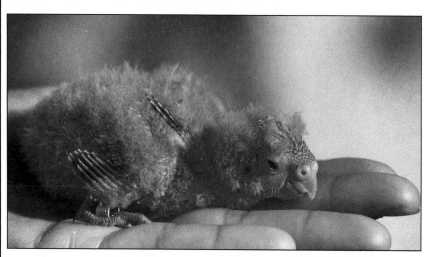

A Mountain Parakeet (*Bolborhynchus aurifrons margaritae*), aged 13 days.

should consist of a mixture of small seeds (such as canary, millet, groats, oats, hemp, and small sunflower seeds), spray millet, seeding grasses, chickweed, dandelion, spinach, carrot, apple, berries, orange, fresh twigs, particularly from pear and apple trees, and – when chicks hatch – bread and milk, or a commercial rearing food.

They will breed in small cages, and a nest box should be permanently available for roosting. The Aymara Parakeet has a large clutch of seven to ten eggs: other members of the genus have a smaller clutch, usually three to five. The incubation period is 23 to 24 days.

Newly hatched chicks are sparingly covered in down, usually white (but recorded as yellowish in one Aymara chick, although others in the same nest had white down). The chicks' eyes open at about 12 days. The young leave the nest after five to six weeks, or up to eight weeks in the Aymara.

Aymara and Lineolated Parakeets have proved very prolific. A pair of the latter, belonging to a British breeder, reared 34 young between November, 1972 and May, 1975 – in a cage.

These little parakeets are very gregarious and breed best within earshot of others of their own genus – or even on the colony system. One London breeder had a successful colony, consisting of three pairs of Lineolated Parakeets, in an outdoor aviary measuring 2.7 m × 76 cm × 1.8 m high (9 ft × 30 in × 6 ft). On one occasion two females shared the same nest box.

The Golden-fronted or Mountain Parakeet (*B. aurifrons*), from Peru, Chile, Argentina, and Bolivia, has proved especially difficult to keep alive in captivity. Most imported birds die within the first weeks or months, gradually losing weight, no matter how well they eat. British veterinarian George Smith found, at *post mortem*, that such birds had suffered from osteomalacia (thinning of the bones). He suggested that they require much higher intensities of sunlight than lowland species, in order to manufacture calciferol. (Andean sunlight is indeed intense.) Early deaths could perhaps be prevented if the diet is supplemented with Vitamin D3.

The two species most likely to be encountered are the Aymara or Sierra Parakeet (*B. aymara*) from Bolivia and Argentina, and the Lineolated Parakeet (*B. lineola*) from southern Mexico, through Central America to Venezuela, Ecuador, and Peru. The Andean Parakeet (*B. orbygnesius*) differs from the Lineolated Parakeet in lacking the barred markings. It originates from Peru. Finally, there is the Rufous-fronted Parakeet (*B. ferrugineifrons*), which is unknown in aviculture. It comes from Colombia.

All members of the genus are quietly colored in shades of green and gray and/or yellow. The Sierra or Aymara has dark gray crown and ear coverts (darker and more extensive in the male), and the sides of the neck and throat are whitish-gray. The male's breast is more silvery-gray – most noticeable in young birds on fledging. The plumage is otherwise mainly green, including the long tail. The

Golden-fronted Parakeet has a slightly shorter tail.

Sexual dimorphism is well marked in the nominate race only. The male has a yellow forehead, lores, cheeks, throat, and part of the breast. In the female, only the cheeks, throat, and the sides of the breast are tinged with yellow. This is very confusing, because in other subspecies the male has similar plumage to that of the female of the nominate race.

The Lineolated Parakeet is most distinctive, with its barred plumage. Most of the feathers of the upper parts have black margins, and there is a black patch on the shoulder. The tail is short and pointed. Its total length is only about 17 cm (6½ in), whereas that of the preceding two species is 18 or 19 cm (about 7 in).

BREEDING

Vast numbers of people who keep parrots consider breeding the most rewarding and interesting aspect of keeping birds. I know of no greater satisfaction than putting together a pair of birds, watching them prepare to nest, witnessing the laying of their eggs, and then observing the development of the chicks. Each newly hatched chick is a fresh miracle whose progress I follow with keen interest. And if it is a rare species, perhaps one that has seldom been raised in captivity, it provides a sense of achievement that nothing else can equal.

Breeding is also important because fewer and fewer birds are caught in the wild and exported. In a few years many species will not be available to aviculturists, unless captive stocks are built up now.

Breeding different parrot species, from the small lovebirds to the large macaws and cockatoos, is achieved under a multitude of different conditions – in small cages or large aviaries, outdoors and indoors.

Success depends on many factors, the most important of which are:
1 The birds must feel secure, and not be threatened or stressed by other birds or outside influences.
2 They must be correctly fed and housed in order to maintain them in the condition where their normal desire to breed is stimulated.
3 They must have a compatible partner – and this must be of the opposite sex! (Many "pairs" ultimately prove to be two males or two females.)
4 They require a suitable nesting site (see *NEST BOXES*).
5 The birds must be suitable for breeding – not too old, inbred, or possessing some physical defect, such as a tumor near the vent, and they must not be unduly nervous.

In many species that breed freely in confinement, such as cockatiels, lovebirds and Australian parakeets, these requirements are easy to fulfill. This is why these species are recommended to the beginner. Starting with "difficult" species is not only discouraging, but does not enable the owner to gain the vital experience needed to be a successful breeder.

The breeder also needs time to observe the birds, to discover if they are incompatible or have problems copulating. There could be a problem as simple as the perch used for copulation being too narrow or placed in an unsuitable position. It is extremely important that owners get to know their birds, and the birds to know them. Successful breeding does not depend on extravagant facilities or even on the most expensive foods, but on a sympathetic keeper.

BROODERS

Brooders are used for chicks that are being hand-reared. Except in warm climates, where a heating pad can supply the warmth necessary to maintain the chick's body temperature, brooders are indispensable.

They should be made of an easily cleaned material, such as melamine. Aquariums can be easily adapted to make excellent brooders. All that is needed is a roof of wood or metal into which are fitted two light bulbs attached to a thermostat, or, if the outside temperature is not likely to fluctuate greatly, to a dimmer (such as is used to dim lights in a room).

In cold climates the sides of the aquarium can be insulated by covering them with polystyrene: ceiling tiles are useful for this purpose. I leave the front uncovered, or, in a brooder specially designed for chicks, have the front made of transparent material.

Conures (2)

Austral Conures
*(Enicognathus
ferruginea minor)* –
two of five young
reared in one nest at
Loro Parque,
Tenerife.

Above: Weddell's, or
the Dusky-headed
Conure *(Aratinga
weddellii)* is found in
Colombia, Ecuador,
Peru, Bolivia, and
Brazil. It is a
free-breeding species
suitable for the
beginner.

The White-eared
Conure *(Pyrrhura
leucotis leucotis)* is
rare in captivity and
endangered in the
wild.

The high price of the Queen of Bavaria's Conure, or Golden Conure (*Aratinga guarouba*), makes it suitable only for experienced breeders.

This brooder is heated by two electric light bulbs in the roof; the bulbs are connected to a room dimmer.

Chicks should be easily observable at all times. They are thus also less nervous than when kept in covered containers. They do like to observe what is going on around them! In addition, if not kept in the dark, they will start to feed at an early age.

Two red 60-W bulbs can be used to heat the brooder. These should be fitted into the roof; underfloor heating can be dangerous, as chicks are too near the heat source. Small chicks should be kept in containers within the brooder. Older chicks are allowed their freedom, on a false floor of welded mesh. On no account should they be kept on wood shavings: many parrot chicks have died as a result of ingesting these.

Newspaper, wood shavings, or any other absorbent material can be placed below the wire-mesh base. Chicks kept on welded mesh are less likely to have foot deformities (such as hind toes pointing forward) than those kept on a soft surface. They can be kept on mesh from the age of a few days.

The brooder should also contain a small spill-proof container of water (to provide some humidity) and a reliable thermometer. The digital type is recommended: it is easy to read and has a probe that can be inserted inside the brooder while the thermometer itself stays outside, thus ensuring it is not fouled by the chicks' droppings.

BUYING

Many mistakes are made in the purchase of parrots, and some are serious enough to deter the buyer from ever trying again. The most common mistakes are:

1 Buying an adult bird for a pet. An inexperienced person can easily be misled into believing that a bird is a youngster. A little research or advice prior to the purchase, or taking the trouble to seek out a reliable breeder of the required species, would prevent this. It is not possible to tame most adult parrots, especially those that are wild-caught.

2 Buying an unsuitable species as a pet. Cockatoos and macaws, for example, are *not* suitable for the average household. It may present a glamorous picture to walk around with a macaw on one's shoulder, but the reality is usually less attractive – a destructive, noisy, demanding bird with which the owner is unable to cope. The result: a neurotic feather-plucking macaw, irate neighbors and a distraught owner. A rare minority of persons have the time, and the essential sympathetic attitude, to keep large parrots at home. Most macaws and cockatoos can live well only in an aviary and with the opportunity to breed.

3 Buying a sick bird. Unfortunately, many wild-caught parrots are fatally diseased, usually as a result of unsanitary conditions in the country of origin prior to being exported. The fact that birds have been quarantined by the importer does not guarantee good health. Regrettably, many imported birds suffer from aspergillosis, salmonella, or even, as the result of overmedication, a diseased liver. They can survive in this condition for several months.

It is always worth paying more to buy a captive-bred young bird from a reputable breeder. There may be a wait of several months for the species desired, but if you choose wisely, your parrot could be your companion for the rest of your life. Impulse buying should be resisted by the inexperienced.

It is most important to look for the following signs of poor health: dull eyes, frequently closed, especially if the bird is

C

sleeping for long periods with fluffed-up plumage and resting on two feet. (Adult birds in good health hold their plumage tightly against their bodies and normally rest on one leg.)

Discharge from the eyes or nostrils, or damp or soiled plumage in this area, are indications of disease. Matted feces, or soiled feathers surrounding the vent are equally serious. Swollen, irritated eyes are a sign of conjunctivitis or a more serious ailment, such as pox.

Avoid birds with labored breathing, accompanied by wheezing sounds or obvious pumping movements of the tail. Examine the mouth to ensure that there are no lesions of candida especially in lories or young birds that have been hand-reared.

Look at the beak. It should not be soft or misshapen. This condition, associated with poor plumage (especially in cockatoos), may indicate that the bird is suffering from *PSITTACINE BEAK AND FEATHER DISEASE SYNDROME* (see entry).

If you intend to buy as a pet an adult bird that is tame and had been a pet in a previous home, be sure to inquire whether the bird prefers men or women. Many will *never* change their preference and will fear and/or attack people of the "wrong" sex.

Be wary of adult birds offered for sale for breeding purposes. There may be a dishonest reason for the sale: the bird may be a killer of females, it may break eggs, be infertile, or too old to reproduce. Pairs of rare species offered for sale are also often suspect. In most instances young birds should be purchased for breeding, because they cannot have already been proved useless in this respect; chances are better for success.

There are many magazines or publications of specialist societies (those dealing with only one group of parrots, such as lovebirds or Amazons) that carry advertisements from breeders. It is mainly young birds that will be offered for sale, whereas adults of unknown history will be found in pet shops.

CAGES

Birdroom Cages

Cages in a birdroom may be used for breeding, for winter accommodation, or for housing young birds. Whatever the purpose, the design will not differ greatly. A principal factor should be ease of cleaning. Suitable materials are melamine and marine plywood that has been stained and varnished; this produces a surface that is easy to wipe clean.

Departing from the traditional type of cage with pull-out trays, a design that I have used in an indoor birdroom can be recommended. The cages measured about 91 cm (3 ft) long, 61 cm (2 ft) deep and 70 cm (28 in) high. Construction was of 19-g, 1.25-cm (½-in) welded mesh on a wooden framework. (The floor can be of a larger size of welded mesh, depending on the feeding habits of the species kept; a larger mesh facilitates cleaning.)

The cages stood on legs 10 cm (4 in) high. They housed small lorikeets, so plastic cat litter trays were used underneath to contain the liquid droppings. For other species newspaper is excellent. The entrance door measured 25 cm (10 in) square. It is important to place this in the center of the cage so that all corners can be reached for cleaning. Nest boxes were attached to the outside of the cage to conserve space within, and for ease of inspection.

Where space is at a premium, cages can be in tiers, reaching from ceiling to floor. This is not an ideal arrangement, but the principal disadvantage of inadequate lighting can easily be overcome. I used a small strip light in each cage, 31 cm (12 in) long, connected at the back of the cages to one cable.

The cages described above are suitable for keeping and breeding lovebirds, *Bolborhynchus* parakeets, and, if cage length is increased, other small neotropical parakeets, such as *Brotogeris* species and others of similar size.

It is worth noting that some birds

The Greater
Sulphur-crested
Cockatoo (*Cacatua
galerita galerita*) – a
pest in Australia, but
cherished and
expensive elsewhere.

Cockatoos (1)

The Umbrella Cockatoo, or White-crested Cockatoo *(Cacatua alba)* from the islands of the Moluccas.

In the Gang Gang Cockatoo *(Callocephalon fimbriatum)* the male is distinguished by his red head.

actually reproduce more successfully in indoor cages than in outdoor aviaries. One species notable in this respect is the little Goldie's Lorikeet (*Trichoglossus goldiei*) from New Guinea.

Pet Cages

Four requirements to bear in mind when choosing a pet bird's cage are that **1** it must be spacious enough for the bird to be able to stretch its wings fully and to move about freely; **2** it should be a suitable shape; **3** it must be easy to clean; and **4** it should have an attractive appearance.

Cages with a plastic base are lighter and easier to keep clean than the traditional type with a tray that slides out. Cages with horizontal bars, which allow the bird to climb more easily, are preferable to those with vertical bars. Plastic perches should be replaced by natural branches, renewed regularly, when the bark has been gnawed off and the surface becomes slippery.

Commercially produced cages for large parrots, such as macaws, are very expensive. Using a 3.6 × 1.8 m (12 × 6 ft) panel of 12-g, 7.5 × 2.5 cm (3 × 1 in) welded mesh, one can build a cage 1.05 m high × 91 cm × 61 cm (3½ × 3 × 2 ft) that is suitable for a single macaw up to the size of a Green-winged.

Cut off 61 cm (2 ft) from the top and the side of the panel and bend the remaining sheet into shape to give the sides of the cage. The 61 cm (2 ft) cutoffs are used to make the roof, floor, and door. The sections can be joined using C-clips for 12-g wire. This cage can be made at a very low cost.

Large mesh such as 7.5 × 2.5 cm (3 × 1 in) is suitable for indoor use, where one does not have to worry about rats, mice, and sparrows gaining entry and stealing the food. The large mesh is more rigid than smaller-mesh wire and therefore easier to work with. Small wire-mesh "legs" can be put under the cage so that newspaper can be laid beneath it.

Suspended Cages

These are ideal for outdoor use in warm climates. They are raised about 1.2 m (4 ft) off the ground and are supported by something like 19 mm (¾ in) galvanized tubing. A framework of this can be constructed to hold any number of cages. The suggested size for medium or small Amazons, *Pionus*, other neotropical parrots and lories is 2.7 × 1 × 1 m high (9 × 3 × 3 ft).

Cockatoos like to be able to walk about on the ground, and Australian parakeets and some other long-tailed species tend to damage their tails in suspended cages. For other species, it is a question of discovering what suits a particular pair of birds.

The sections of wire used in construction can be joined by C-clips, or by folding the protruding wire, where the mesh is cut, around the piece of mesh to which it is to be joined. If 16 g, 2.5 × 2.5 cm (1 × 1 in) welded mesh is used, it supports itself without sagging. Longer cages than the size suggested will need to be strengthened, using angle irons.

To provide protection from wind, rain, and sun, part of the sides and roof can be covered in opaque material that is pop riveted onto the framework. There must be a door at each end to facilitate catching, which can be difficult in suspended cages. This is the main disadvantage.

A cage for a pet bird, such as this cockatiel, must be spacious enough for the bird to extend its wings fully and to move around freely. Note that the plastic perches have been replaced by natural perches that are much better for the bird's feet.

These cages are more hygienic than others, in that the feces fall through the wire base of the cage, as do small items of uneaten food. The floor can be kept clean by hosing and scraping. It is often stated that birds feel more secure in suspended cages because no one can enter their territory, but the main point in favor of suspended cages, from the keeper's point of view, is the reduced time spent in cleaning and maintenance.

CAIQUES (*Pionites*)

Few more distinctive or delightful genera of parrots exist. Caiques are recognized by their white breast, contrasting with green upper parts and orange or yellow thighs. The stance is unusually upright and the tails are square. There is no marked sexual dimorphism. Caiques originate from the Amazon basin and the northern part of South America (Guianas, Brazil, Colombia, Peru, Ecuador, and northern Bolivia).

Two species are recognized, the only difference being pigmentation. The Black-headed Caique (*P. melanocephala*) has the top of the head and the feet and beak black, and the White-bellied Caique (*P. leucogaster*) has the top of the head pale orange and the feet and beak pale pinkish. In length these are 23 cm (9 in).

The subspecies *pallida* differs from the Black-headed Caique mainly in having the thighs yellow, not orange, and *xanthomeria* differs from the White-bellied Caique in having the thighs and flanks yellow instead of green. There is also a caique from northwestern Brazil, (*P. l. xanthurus*) that has the entire tail yellow. It is almost unknown in captivity.

Behaviorally, caiques are among the most fascinating of parrots. They display and vocalize loudly at the slightest provocation, in a shrill, penetrating voice. The display is similar to that of some conures, but more exaggerated: they lean forward on the perch and sway their bodies in a circular motion, opening and vibrating the wings at great speed so that they appear a blur, and dilate their pupils so that they blaze red-orange.

Caiques have a great need to gnaw and should be provided with fresh green branches every week. Kept in a small group, they are extremely interesting to watch, but once the group is established, no newcomer should be added. They act as one, investigating, feeding, and playing, in a manner that is a great pleasure to observe. Colony breeding of Black-headed Caiques is not advised, because they are usually too aggressive, or one male will become dominant and take over all the females.

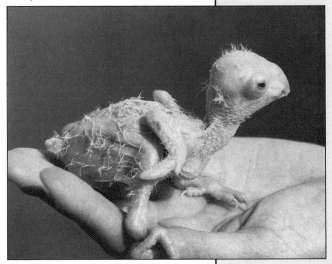

A Yellow-thighed Caique (*Pionites leucogaster xanthomeria*), aged 23 days.

With the White-bellied Caique, however, colony breeding can be extremely successful. At Busch Gardens, Tampa, Florida, the colony on exhibit for many years produced numerous young. All the birds used the same large nest box for roosting and breeding. At one time four females were raising as many as seven young!

Caiques are being bred with increasing frequency, but still in small numbers. They are seldom imported these days; thus captive breeding is very important. Probably the most successful breeder of the Black-headed Caique, Tom Ireland, resides in Florida. When his pairs were separated by other neotropical species, the results were poor; when moved into adjacent cages, production increased dramatically. The cages are very small, approximately 46 × 91 × 91 cm high (1½ × 3 × 3 ft) and suspended about 91 cm (3 ft) off the ground. There are no solid partitions between these all-wire cages. The first female will lay at the end of December and within a couple of weeks most of the other pairs will also be incubating eggs.

The diet of these birds does not differ from that of the other parrots in Tom Ireland's collection. Food consists of a mixture of various dry seeds, large quantities of fresh corn on the cob, other vegetables and fruits, and a mixture of whole-grain bread, grated carrot, and endive. Caiques are extremely fond of fruit and need more than almost any other parrot.

They relish cracked walnuts and cubes of cheese, and some will take bread and milk when rearing young.

Three to four eggs are laid, incubated by the female. The incubation period is usually 25 days. The young spend about ten weeks in the nest.

Callocephalon fimbriatum – see *GANG GANG COCKATOO*

Chalcopsitta LORIES

The four lories that comprise this genus have totally contrasting basic colors (black, brown, green, and red). These birds are large, with long, broad tails, their total length being approximately 30 cm (12 in). The skin surrounding the lower mandible is naked (this is also the case with the Dusky Lory, *Pseudeos fuscata*).

The diet consists of nectar and fruit. Corn on the cob and sweetcorn kernels will be eaten by most *Chalcopsitta* species, especially those with young. Some will also consume bread and milk and mealworms. Many newly imported birds are very conservative feeders.

Imported *Chalcopsitta* lories take three or four years to become sexually mature; captive-bred birds mature more quickly. Two eggs are laid and the incubation period is 24 days. These lories may be single- or double-brooded, depending on climate and whether the young are removed for hand-rearing. Once they start to breed they often prove prolific, but many pairs apparently lack the stimulus or correct conditions to induce breeding.

Three species come from New Guinea.

The Black Lory (*C. atra*) is black with a purple sheen and a blue sheen on the rump. The underside of the tail is red and yellow. Immature birds may have a few, or many, red feathers on any part of the head or body. Bare facial skin is white in young birds and black in adults.

One of the most unusually colored of all parrots is

Duivenbode's Lory (*Chalcopsitta duivenbodei*) – a chick aged 52 days.

Duivenbode's Lory (*C. duivenbodei*). The basic color is brown with a golden tinge; the narrow, elongated feathers on the neck are yellow, and the thighs and entire underwing coverts are golden yellow. A striking area of feathers, encircling beak and throat, are also golden yellow. A beautiful contrast is provided by the violet-blue lower back, rump, and undertail coverts. Immature birds are much duller, with shorter tails and the facial skin white.

The third member of the genus from New Guinea is the Yellow-streaked Lory (*C. scintillata*). The forehead and crown (or forehead only) are red, and also the thighs and underwing coverts. The upper parts are mainly green and the lower back sky blue. The underparts are brownish on the breast and green on the abdomen, the whole being prominently streaked with yellow. Shaft-streaking (the prominent streak in the center of the feather) reaches maximum development in this species. Immature birds are much duller, with black instead of red on much of the head, or with a more brownish coloration overall. Full bright adult plumage takes several years to acquire. Mature birds are gaudy but very beautiful.

The Cardinal Lory (*C. cardinalis*) from the Solomon Islands is very rare in captivity, because few birds are exported from those islands. It is, however, common in the wild. Entirely red, with brownish-red on the wings and breast, it has tiny silvery feathers on the bend of the wing. The small beak is red in adults, and brownish in immature birds. The skin surrounding the beak is yellow and black. There is no shaft-streaking in this species.

Charmosyna LORIES

The members of this genus can be divided into two groups – those that have the underparts mainly red, and those in which the plumage is basically green. Four of the 14 species are reasonably well known in aviculture; the others are virtually unknown. These lories are found in New Guinea and various islands of the Moluccas (Indonesia) and the Pacific.

In captivity, these lories are even more reliant on nectar than other lories, but most will also eat some fruit. Only rarely is seed taken; my own *placentis* relish spray millet. (See *NECTAR*.)

Most members of the genus are small, and all are slender, finely proportioned birds. The largest is Stella's Lorikeet (*C. papou stellae*), which is slightly larger in body size than a Perfect Lorikeet (*Trichoglossus euteles*). The unique feature of Stella's (for a lory) is the great length of the tail. It seems that this increases with age. In a male known to be at least ten years old, the tail is approximately 38 cm (15 in) long – that is nearly twice the length of the body.

After watching Stella's Lorikeet for a few seconds, I am always convinced that this is the most beautiful bird in the world. It has extreme grace of form, stunning color, no loud or discordant notes, but only intriguing, distinctive vocalizations, sexual dimorphism, and the longest, fluttering tail of any parrot. Few birds are more fascinating to watch. Stella's Lorikeets make darting movements of the body without moving the feet, jump effortlessly over a companion and, in display, perform exaggerated circular swaying movements.

Unfortunately, their extreme beauty has resulted in their being favored above all other birds, except birds of paradise, for tribal decoration by New Guinea tribesmen. Whole skins are used,

and the females, with daffodil yellow rump and sides, are probably especially sought after. The male is red in these areas. (Young birds can be sexed in nest feather.) Unusually, there is a melanistic phase that is as common as the red. In this phase the red areas are replaced by black. Two melanistic birds paired together can produce melanistic and red young.

Two eggs are laid. The incubation period is 26 days and the young spend between seven and eight weeks in the nest.

Almost similar to Stella's Lorikeet in coloration is the Josephine's Lorikeet (*C. josefinae*). It has a red tail, lacks the central elongated feathers and is slightly smaller. The lower back is yellow in the female, and red in the male. This species has a less extravert personality.

Both the foregoing are found in New Guinea, as is the much smaller Fairy Lorikeet (*C. pulchella*). It measures about 18 cm (7 in). Mainly green above and red below, the male has the undertail coverts red and yellow; in the female they are greenish-yellow, as are the sides of the rump. There are yellow streaks on the upper breast (on a background of green in the subspecies *rothschildi*).

The Fairy Lorikeet has not often been imported and has seldom bred in captivity. It cannot tolerate low temperatures, and thus, rather than move pairs indoors during cold weather, it may be advisable to keep them indoors permanently or, better still, in a small heated, planted house. Here they are seen at their best.

Under the right conditions they should prove prolific; if one nest fails, more eggs will be laid after about three weeks. This is a totally delightful little bird that deserves the attention of specialist breeders prepared to go to some trouble to establish a species in captivity.

The foregoing remarks apply equally to the Pleasing or Red-flanked Lorikeet (*C. placentis*). One specialist Danish breeder found exactly the right conditions for this most attractive little bird, and reared 40 in four years. He used a heated, glass-fronted cage in an indoor birdroom.

As with the other members of the genus known in captivity,

incubation is shared by male and female. The young spend about 56 days in the nest and can be sexed as soon as they feather (males have red flanks). The Red-flanked Lorikeet occurs in New Guinea, Indonesia (Moluccas), and the Solomon Islands (Bougainville).

Note that the respiration rate in the small *Charmosyna* species is noticeably more rapid than in other small parrots.

CHICKS
Parrot chicks are altricial – that is, on hatching they are totally helpless, are fed by the parents, and have their eyes and ears closed. They may be virtually naked but for a few wisps of down (*Eclectus*, *Psittacula*), or have a small amount of down (*Aratinga* conures), or be densely covered (some lories, *Calyptorhynchus* cockatoos).

The variation in development among the genera is great: the period they spend in the nest varies between only four and a half weeks (*Forpus* parrotlets, budgerigars) and four months (large macaws and cockatoos). For example, Amazon (*Amazona*) parrots, which spend about eight to ten weeks in the nest, weigh between 8–10 g (2–3½ oz) on hatching, according to the species. They have only a few wisps of down. The eyes open at about three weeks and the ears a few days later. The plumage is almost complete by about two months. There is little second down, whereas some parrots (lories and

Eclectus, for example) are heavily clothed in second down by three to four weeks of age. The down color varies from white to light gray, dark gray, or even yellow.

CHICKS, FAILURE TO FEED
There are three basic reasons why birds fail to feed their chicks at all, or suddenly cease to feed them. The first is inexperience. A pair of birds that have never hatched young before sometimes starve their first chicks. Subsequently they may prove to be good parents.

The second reason is that the chick has become chilled or is sick. A chick that is too weak to hold up its head to receive food cannot be fed by the parents.

On occasion, an experienced pair will cease to feed a chick that is apparently quite healthy. If this chick is removed and hand-fed, often it will not thrive because there is something fundamentally wrong with it. The parents knew this instinctively! Experienced parents usually have a good reason for deserting a chick.

Thirdly, a pair may cease to feed any of their young because of some stressful environmental disturbance. Examples are disturbance by cats or vermin at night, severe weather conditions, or some unusual happening or loud noise in the vicinity of the aviary. Nest inspection should not cause desertion, except just possibly in the case of very nervous birds whose nest has not previously been examined.

Macaw chicks, such as this Blue and Yellow (*Ara ararauna*), are among the most appealing of young birds.

CITES

This is the abbreviation for the Convention on International Trade in Endangered Species of Wild Fauna and Flora. Sooner or later the reader will find this mentioned in avicultural literature, as it increasingly affects the availability of species. For the purpose of this Convention, which monitors trade, all species of parrots are placed in one of three categories, Appendix I, II, or III, according to whether the species is endangered, threatened, or not at risk, respectively.

Representatives from countries throughout the world that are signatories to CITES meet every year and propose additions to, or removals from, the various appendixes. A vote is taken on the evidence offered to decide whether additions or deletions should be made. In most cases, little information is available on population numbers, only that the population is declining and that it must be protected from trade.

Applications to import or export species on Appendix I or II have to be made to the appropriate authority of the exporting country and each case is decided individually. It may take up to three months to obtain the necessary permission to export an endangered species. Those imported without the necessary documentation are confiscated by Customs if recognized.

The name of the department that deals with CITES documentation can be obtained by writing to the Secretariat of CITES, 6 rue de Maupas, Case Postale 78, CH 1000 Lausanne 9, Switzerland.

At the time of going to press, the following parrot species were listed in Appendix I (endangered):

Amazona arausiaca
   barbadensis
   brasiliensis
   dufresniana rhodocorytha
   guildingii
   imperialis
   leucocephala
   pretrei
   tucumana
   versicolor
   vinacea
   vittata
Anodorhynchus hyacinthinus
   *leari**
Ara ambigua
   glaucogularis
   macao
   maracana
   militaris
   rubrogenys
Aratinga guarouba
Cacatua moluccensis
Cyanopsitta spixii
Cyanoramphus auriceps forbesi
   novaezelandiae
Geopsittacus occidentalis
Neophema chrysogaster
Ognorhynchus icterotis
Opopsitta diophthalma coxeni
Pezoporus wallicus
Pionopsitta pileata
Probosciger aterrimus
Psephotus chrysopterygius
   pulcherrimus (presumed
   extinct)
Psittacula eques
Psittacus erithacus princeps
Pyrrhura cruentata
Rhynchopsitta pachyrhyncha
   terrisi
Strigops habroptilus

All other species of parrots are listed in Appendix II (threatened), with the exception of *Melopsittacus undulatus* (budgerigar or parakeet, *Nymphicus hollandicus* (cockatiel) and *Psittacula krameri* (Ringneck Parakeet). Those who obtain birds imported with CITES papers must ensure that these papers are retained. Without them it may be difficult or impossible to re-export or sell the birds.

(*also *Anodorhynchus glaucus* if extant)

CLUTCH

A clutch is the term for the number of eggs laid in one breeding period. In parrots it varies from one in the Black Cockatoos (sometimes two), two in Eclectus Parrots, most lories and some cockatoos, three or four in Amazons, *Pionus*, and macaws, and four, five, or up to eight in most Australian parakeets.

The usual clutch size of some other parakeets is larger; the little *Bolborhynchus aymara*, for example, usually lays eight to ten eggs. Perhaps this indicates that the normal lifespan of the species is short, or possibly that they breed only under optimum conditions that may not occur every year.

The abnormally large clutches recorded in some Australian species, such as cockatiels and parakeets – up to 12 eggs – may be the result of domestication. In the wild these species breed only when conditions are favorable, i.e., after rain, when there is an ample supply of food on which to rear their young. Captive birds normally have abundant supplies of food.

In most parrots, eggs are laid every second or third day. In some small species the interval may be as short as 36 hours, and in some large ones (notably cockatoos) the interval could be four or five days.

The difference in clutch size between closely related species can be explained by their habitats. More food is available per bird in habitats where there are seasonal fluctuations of climate and plant growth (most of the Australian parakeets originate from such areas) and, therefore, here the inhabitants lay larger clutches than those from rain forest, for example. In the latter type of habitat, there are no well-marked seasons and availability of food does not vary greatly throughout the year. There is no sudden increase in food supply, therefore clutch sizes are smaller.

In some birds, known as indeterminate layers, the clutch size can be influenced. If eggs are removed when laid, a larger number of eggs than normal will be produced. Owners of single pet budgies, for example, often make the mistake of removing any eggs that are laid, instead of allowing the bird to incubate them. The result is that an enormous number of eggs are laid, possibly severely debilitating the female, or even resulting in her death if adequate calcium is not supplied for egg production.

Other species lay a predetermined number of eggs in one clutch; these are known as determinate layers and their clutch size cannot be influenced by the removal of eggs.

The number of clutches laid per year also varies. At one extreme there are the almost continuous layers, such as lovebirds (*Agapornis*) and Eclectus Parrots, who will lay again within about three weeks of the eggs or young being removed. Others, such as lories, lay several clutches in the course of one year. Some birds are double-brooded or single-brooded, while others – Amazons, for example – normally lay only one clutch if this proves successful in producing young.

(See also *EGGS*.)

COCKATIEL (*Nymphicus hollandicus*)

The cockatiel is immensely popular with breeders and pet-bird keepers. It is not a parakeet, as its long tail leads many to believe, but is very closely related to the cockatoos. This is apparent from its breeding behavior (male and female take turns in incubating the eggs, for example) and in the appearance of the chicks before they are feathered.

There can be no finer bird to introduce beginners to parrot keeping. Simple to feed, hardy, sexable at a glance, easy to breed, low-priced, long-lived, yet ready to breed at a year old – what more could anyone ask in one bird? It has a pleasant warbling "song" – which, incidentally, can be used as an indication of sex at an early age (young males start to warble at about three months old).

In recent years the development of numerous attractive color mutations has enormously increased the cockatiel's popularity with bird fanciers and this has led to thousands discovering that the cockatiel is one of the most wonderful pets. Pretty, intelligent, affectionate, easily tamed and a good mimic of words and whistled tunes, no pet bird gives more enjoyment to a family. Its small size makes it easy and safe for a child to handle, yet being twice the body size of a budgerigar, it is a step towards the larger parrots.

Cockatiels originate from Australia, where they occur over most of the continent except for coastal areas. Their natural diet consists almost entirely of seeds, and thus they have adapted well to captivity. None have been exported from Australia for many years: all those available have been captive-bred for generations.

More than one third of the cockatiel's total length of 31 cm (13 in) consists of the tail. Its weight is in the region of 90 g (3 oz). The wild-type bird, from which the mutations have been developed, is mainly gray with the head yellow and a prominent patch of orange on the ear coverts (without which it would be not nearly as attractive). This patch is brighter in the male, as is, normally, the yellow crest. The large white patch on the wing is not fully evident until the bird is seen in flight.

In adult birds, another prominent difference between the sexes is the coloration of the underside of the tail: black in males, and barred with yellow and gray in the female. Young birds resemble females, but have much shorter tails and pinkish ceres.

The most popular mutation is the lutino (often called white, or even albino, but neither of these names is technically correct). It is mainly white or pale yellow (deeper yellow in strains in which breeders have concentrated on color) with the orange and yellow facial markings retained. This mutation is difficult to sex. Males have a few irregular yellow marks on the underside of wings and tail. In adult females, and in immature birds of both sexes, these areas are faintly, but regularly, barred with yellow.

Several other mutations and countless combinations of mutations (such as cinnamon pearl pied) are being bred. (The breeder who is especially interested in color mutations is advised to obtain a book on breeding cockatiels.) Mutations include the pied (specialist breeders aim for a bird that is mainly pale yellow with gray on the wings), cinnamon and cinnamon pied (the gray markings are replaced by soft fawn), silver (very light gray) and pearl.

The dietary requirements of cockatiels are easily satisfied. They need a seed mixture that consists of canary seed, millet, and oats or groats, and a little sunflower, with the addition of a little hemp and niger during cold weather. Alternatively, budgerigar mixture can be offered in one container and a little sunflower seed in another. Spray millet is relished at all times. Every day some greens should be offered: chickweed, seeding grasses, kale, spinach, and other greens, such as the leafy part of celery. Some cockatiels will eat a little apple and carrot.

Breeding birds need a nutritious rearing food, such as whole grain bread and milk, or a drier mixture made from bread, hard-boiled egg, and grated carrot, for example. Some will eat the commercial egg foods made for canaries.

COCKATOOS (*Cacatua* and *Eolophus*)

Any layperson can recognize a cockatoo – a white, crested parrot – but not all cockatoos are white. Several species are black (see *BLACK COCKATOOS*). Two species from Australia have a lot of pink in their body plumage.

One of these, the Roseate, Rose-breasted, or Galah Cockatoo (*Eolophus* or *Cacatua roseicapillus*), is generally considered distinct enough in behavior and appearance to warrant a separate genus. It is gray above and pink below.

Leadbeater's or Major Mitchell's Cockatoo (*C. leadbeateri*) is also pink below but easily recognized by the spectacular bands of orange in its crest. This is often considered to be the most beautiful of the white cockatoos.

Cockatoo chicks grow slowly: at 47 days this Umbrella Cockatoo (*Cacatua alba*) was only half feathered. It weighed 452 g (1 lb).

SPECIES	APPROX LENGTH*		BEAK	DISTINGUISHING FEATURES	ORIGIN
	cm	in			
Greater Sulphur-crested (*C. galerita galerita*)	54	21	black	yellow crest – narrow feathers	Australia
Triton (*C. g. triton*)	47	18	black	yellow crest – broader feathers	New Guinea, Indonesia
Blue-eyed (*C. ophthalmica*)	50	19	black	broad yellow crest feathers, brighter blue skin around eye	New Britain, New Ireland
† Lesser Sulphur-crested (*C. sulphurea sulphurea*)	33	12½	black	yellow crest – narrow feathers, ear coverts yellow	Indonesia, including Celebes, Sunda
† Timor (*C. s. parvula*)	30	12	black	smaller beak, slimmer body	Indonesia, including Djampea
† Citron-crested (*C. s. citrinocristata*)	34	13	black	orange crest – narrow feathers, faint orange ear coverts	Sunda, Indonesia
† Umbrella (White-crested) (*C. alba*)	46	18	black	white crest – very broad feathers	northern and central Indonesia
Moluccan (Salmon-crested) (*C. moluccensis*)	50	20	black	spectacular salmon crest, long, broad feathers	southern Moluccan Islands, Indonesia
Bare-eyed (Little Corella) (*C. sanguinea sanguinea* or *C. pastinator sanguinea*)	36	14	whitish-gray	gray-blue skin surrounding eye – more below; short white crest, orange-pink at base	northern Australia
Western Long-billed Corella (*C. pastinator pastinator* or *C. tenuirostris pastinator*)	39	16	whitish-gray	deep salmon feathers on forehead and lores, short white crest	southwestern Australia
Slender-billed (*C. tenuirostris tenuirostris*)	39	16	whitish-gray	As in *pastinator*, but with salmon feathers on upper breast	southeastern Australia
† Goffins's (*C. goffini*)	31	13	whitish-gray	short white crest, orange-pink at base of crest and on lores, circular white skin around eye	Tenimber Islands
† Philippine Red-vented (*C. haematuropygia*)	32	13	whitish-gray	undertail coverts red, short white crest	Philippine Islands
† Ducorp's (*C. ducorpsi*)	35	14	whitish-gray	white crest, broad feathers, blue skin around eye	Solomon Islands

* There can be considerable size variation within a species.
† Male: iris black/female: iris brown or reddish-brown.

Identification of the other species can be difficult (see the table).

Although many cockatoos are kept as pets, their reign indoors is seldom long. Their loud voices and ability to destroy anything in sight result in most ending up in an aviary.

They *must* have constant occupation for their beaks; part of a fresh-cut branch should be given to a caged cockatoo every day, and also something hard, like a leather dog chew toy, or a strong chain. If normal food and water containers prove inadequate, because of the strength and playfulness of a cockatoo, large earthenware dog bowls can be used.

Diet should be as recommended for Amazons, although many cockatoos will consume more greens (even stalks of cabbage, cauliflower and the stalk and center from peppers). Much may be wasted, but the birds do enjoy shredding these vegetables. In addition, cockatoos should have nuts. The large species can crack whole Brazils and walnuts; the smaller ones enjoy cracked or halved nuts, and also pine nuts and peanuts.

Breeding cockatoos is a challenge. Sexing is easy in those species in which the male has a black iris and the female a brown or red-brown iris. A serious problem (more common in *galerita*, *sulphurea*, *ducorpsi* and *leadbeateri*) is that the male often attacks the female because she is not in breeding condition. Such attacks can be swift and fatal, sometimes resulting in the female's upper mandible being torn off. It can happen in long-established, or newly introduced pairs. For this reason, it may be advisable to cut the male's flight feathers before introducing the female.

Unlike most male parrots, white cockatoos share incubation, usually carrying out this task during the day. The clutch consists of two to four eggs that are incubated for about 28 days. The young remain in the nest for ten, 11, or sometimes 12 weeks. Animal protein should be included in the

40

diet while young are being reared.

The Roseate Cockatoo differs from other cockatoos in its short incubation period (23 days) and in that its young leave the nest at seven weeks. The clutch size is usually two to four eggs, but can be up to six eggs.

CONSERVATION

In recent years the habitats of many parrot species, especially those occurring in rain forest, have been greatly reduced, even almost totally destroyed. This applies particularly to those birds inhabiting islands (notably the Caribbean and certain Indonesian islands), southeastern Brazil, and many other areas of South and Central America, and other parts of the tropics where recent development has been rapid. It applies not only to Third World countries but even to Australia where forests are destroyed to make way for agriculture. In New Guinea, for example, development is relatively recent, but will endanger the existence of many bird species within the next couple of decades. Some parrots can adapt to an altered habitat and live in agricultural areas or secondary forest, but many other species cannot adapt and are doomed to extinction unless destruction of their habitat ceases.

For a number of species it is already too late. On the Indian Ocean island of Mauritius, the native Echo Parakeet (*Psittacula eques*), found nowhere else, has already been reduced to the last dozen representatives of its species, because it can live only in its native habitat, most of which was destroyed by the early 1970s. A belated program was initiated to attempt to save it, but when the population of a species has been reduced to only double figures, such action is usually far too late.

In some instances captive breeding can play a very valuable part in conservation. Unfortunately, most highly endangered parrot species have too few representatives in captivity (or even none at all) for this to be possible. However, some Amazons, conures, and *Cyanoramphus* parakeets will almost certainly be saved from extinction by captive breeding.

It may be that there are already more examples of some species in captivity than in the wild. Certain Australian parakeets, that are nomadic and inhabit the remote interior are so little known that their current status cannot be recorded accurately. Thus, captive populations at least ensure the continued existence of the species, although many conservationists argue that multigeneration captive-breeding alters a species to the point where it is so far removed from its wild counterpart that it could not survive if reintroduced to the wild. Undoubtedly this is correct in some instances.

In other cases, however, captive-breeding over a short term can be used to increase the numbers of a threatened species quite rapidly. Only if suitable habitat existed could captive-bred birds be returned to the wild, but it is precisely because their habitat has been destroyed that they are endangered. In a few cases the combined pressures of trade and deforestation have caused the decline. In recent years international legislation (see *CITES*) has ensured that trade will no longer threaten the existence of species, but such legislation cannot be totally effective until signed and upheld by most countries.

CONURE

Conure is the name given to certain genera of parakeets from South and Central America. Members of the *Aratinga*, *Pyrrhura*, and *Cyanoliseus* genera are invariably known as conures, whereas the two species of the genus *Enicognathus* can be known either as conures or parakeets; for example, Slender-billed Conure or Slender-billed Parakeet.

Conures have a reputation for being noisy and destructive. This is true of the larger species, but not of the *Pyrrhuras*. All are very interesting aviary birds, many are free-breeding and most make exceptionally good parents. Young birds make enchanting, affectionate, and intelligent pets, their main drawback being that they shriek for attention in a voice that is far from pleasant.

See also: *Aratinga CONURES*, *Enicognathus CONURES*, *Nandayus CONURE*, *PATAGONIAN CONURE*, and *Pyrrhura CONURES*.

Coracopsis **PARROTS** – See *VASA PARROTS*

CRIMSON-WINGED PARAKEETS (*Aprosmictus*)

The two parakeets in this genus are distinctive birds of great beauty. They are mainly green with red in the wings. Their appearance is neat and the tail longish and broad. In length they are about 32 cm (13 in).

The Australian Crimson-winged Parakeet (*A. erythropterus*) is well established in captivity and a favorite with many breeders. The male is an exceptionally handsome bird – and unmistakable, being the only parakeet to have shining black on its back. The lower back is blue. The female is almost entirely green with a narrower area of red along the length of the wing.

In both sexes the beak is red in adults and yellowish in young birds. Immature birds resemble the female. Adult plumage is acquired during the third year, but males usually show some black feathers on the mantle at about 18 months.

It is found in northern and eastern Australia, as far south as northern New South Wales, and in southern New Guinea. Its diet in the wild includes the seeds of eucalyptus and acacia, fruits, berries, nuts, insects and nectar.

Traditional, rather than suspended, aviaries are recommended. In length they should be in the region of 3.6–4.2 m (12–14 ft). When the young are due to fledge, they must be protected from flying at speed into the wire by placing a mass of branches at the end of the aviary. Crimson-winged Parakeets greatly enjoy rain bathing, so part of the roof should be of wire only.

A varied seed mixture should be offered, containing sunflower, safflower, canary, buckwheat, oats, white millet, and, in cold weather, a little niger and linseed. Peanuts, small pine nuts, and spray millet are relished. Fresh fruit and vegetables should be offered daily, especially chickweed, sowthistle, seeding grasses, spinach, celery, and carrot, as well as apple and orange. Berries from hawthorn and elder are favorites, and some Crimson-wings will also eat blackberries.

They start to breed at three years. As they are often early nesters, the box should be in position by February. It should measure approximately 31 cm (1 ft) square and 61 cm (2 ft) high. Some breeders have found that withholding the nest until, say, April, when the weather might be more favorable, has resulted in the birds not nesting at all. Three to six eggs are laid, but the number is usually four or five. The incubation period is 21 days.

Newly hatched chicks are thickly covered with white down that is replaced by gray down by the age of about ten days. By three weeks they are feathering up, with red and green wing feathers erupting. They leave the nest between five and six weeks of age.

Nest inspection should be carried out daily, as soon after first light as possible, especially with pairs that have not hatched chicks previously. The main danger is that the female might cease to brood the young at night, before they can maintain their body temperature. This is the principal reason for death in chicks found with food in their crops. If the nest is inspected early in the day there is a chance that chilled chicks can be saved. Males usually help to feed the chicks that are still in the nest.

A watch must be kept for signs of aggression in males that are trying to drive the female to nest. To prevent injury to the female, it may be necessary to clip the male's wings. The Crimson-winged Parakeet may seem an unlikely subject for a colony aviary, yet one well-known aviculturist has an aviary containing six pairs; it measures 9 × 4.5 × 2.7 m high (30 × 15 × 9 ft). No serious fighting has occurred.

The Timor Crimson-winged Parakeet (*A. jonquillaceus*) has less striking but more subtle coloration. It is a much lighter, more delicate shade of green, with a dark green mantle and upper back. The male has the margins of these feathers in blue, and also a blue bend of the wing. The female lacks the blue margins and has a green bend of the wing. Some of the wing coverts are yellow, tinged with green. In the smaller subspecies *wetterensis*, these wing coverts are green, slightly suffused with yellow.

D

DIET

Diet, environment (including temperature), hygiene, and avoidance of stress are the most important factors for a long and healthy life in captive parrots. Of these, diet is the most easily controlled, and careful attention must be paid to it. Variety in the diet is extremely important, and with some birds (especially wild-caught), it is often necessary to persevere for a long period, possibly several years, to achieve this. A bias towards one item of food, such as sunflower seed, can result in dietary deficiencies, obesity and even damage to internal organs such as the liver. If a bird's diet consisted of 60% sunflower seed or some other acceptable item of food, this would be unlikely to prove harmful provided that the other 40% consisted of a variety of foods, including fresh fruits and vegetables. These are an important source of Vitamins A and B, which are essential for good health. (See also *SEED, SUNFLOWER*.)

The diet of many species can include items from the table, which, if sensibly chosen, are nourishing and beneficial. Owners should not worry unduly if their pets prefer to eat cooked meat and vegetables, rice, pasta, bread, crackers, and other biscuits and cakes. They could live on this indefinitely and be a lot healthier than a parrot that had to exist solely on dry seed.

It is very important to experiment, because no two parrots have the same preferences where food is concerned. Except with small species, some items are almost universally popular – cracked walnuts, hawthorn berries, corn on the cob, grapes, and pomegranates; few birds, whatever their size, will refuse spray millet.

In addition to variety, an obviously important aspect of correct feeding is the suitability of the items offered. It is no good giving seed to Pesquet's Parrots, nectar to macaws, or nuts to lories. Whereas many species are omnivorous, others are specialist feeders and *must* have the correct food if they are to survive. In my opinion, parrots should have food in front of them at all times; they should not be rationed. Neither should the diet consist largely of manufactured foods, such as pellets. These are very satisfactory for poultry, but not for parrots, whose enjoyment of foods of different types, textures and flavors should be supremely evident to any caring owner. They receive no enjoyment – and no essential wear on the beak – from such artificial fare.

(See also *FRUITS, GRIT, NECTAR, PROTEIN* and *VEGETABLES.*)

DUSKY LORY– see *Pseudeos LORY*

Aim for variety in the diet, especially with fresh fruits and vegetables.

E

ECLECTUS PARROTS

Eclectus Parrots have three great assets that have assured their popularity as aviary birds: they are spectacularly colorful, sexually dimorphic (they can be sexed at three and a half weeks old!), and nest readily. They originate from Australia, New Guinea, and Indonesia, although most of those now available are captive-bred.

An Eclectus chick.

There is only one species of Eclectus, but recognition of the seven subspecies is difficult in the males, which do not differ greatly. The main differences are in length: 31–38 cm (12–15 in), in shade of green, and whether or not the tail is tipped with yellow.

Females differ significantly, and the principal features used for recognition are as follows:

1 a narrow circle of blue feathers surrounding the eye, as in the Red-sided (*E. r. polychloros*), *E. r. macgillivrayi* from northern Australia, which is not likely to be encountered outside that country, and in the smallest race, *solomonensis*, which is not common in captivity;

2 absence of blue on the underparts (all red) as in *cornelia* and the larger *riedeli*;

3 yellow in the tail and lacking blue feathers around the eye, as in the nominate race and *vosmaeri*, two of the larger subspecies.

Immature birds can be distinguished by the grayish iris and by the bill color, which is brownish.

Eclectus have long been among my own favorites. Many become very tame and even aviary birds will mimic sounds around them, including a few words. Young ones readily learn to talk, some even without tuition. However, the females tend to be bad-tempered and are definitely not recommended as pets. Breeding pairs can be kept in suspended cages or traditional aviaries.

The measurements of the nest box should be about 31 cm (1 ft) square and 61 cm (2 ft) high. In some pairs females are dominant and could keep the male away from the food; two feeding points should be provided if there is any hint of this, especially in newly introduced birds.

It is quite usual for females to spend most of their lives inside the nest once they are sexually mature. One clutch follows another, within about three weeks if the first was not successful, or after removal of the young. The two eggs are incubated for 28 days and the young spend 10 to 11 weeks in the nest.

Very important is an abundance of fresh vegetables and fruits, and also berries such as hawthorn and elder. Deprived of sufficient Vitamin A, Eclectus will contract candidiasis (lesions may be seen in the mouth). Carrots and tomatoes are good sources of this vitamin, or a multivitamin supplement (most of which have a high Vitamin A content) may be added to a favorite item of food, or to bread and milk.

Most Eclectus will eat many small seeds, such as white millet, canary, and hemp, in addition to sunflower and safflower seeds, spray millet, peanuts, and pine nuts. Celery, cubes of cheese, and corn on the cob are favored items.

Some Eclectus can be very noisy – enough to disturb neighbors – but individuals vary considerably in this respect.

A newly hatched Salvadori's Fig Parrot (*Psittaculirostris salvadorii*).

secreted from a gland in the uterus. The shell of a fertile egg becomes thinner during the incubation period, because the chick draws on the shell's calcium for its own skeletal growth. A thin-shelled egg is therefore unlikely to produce a viable chick. It may also cause the female to become eggbound.

The range of size and weight in parrot eggs is obviously great. In the Spectacled Parrotlet (*Forpus conspicillatus*), for example, a female weighs about 25 g (1 oz), and the new-laid egg weighs about 1 g (.03 oz) and measures approximately 16 × 15 mm (5/8 × 5/8 in). In a Moluccan Cockatoo, the adult weighs about 800 g (28 oz), the egg weighs about 25 g (1 oz), and measures 44 × 32 mm (1¾ × 1¼ in). Young birds, laying for the first time, and old birds tend to lay smaller eggs than birds of optimum breeding age.

(See also *CLUTCH*.)

EGGS

All parrot eggs are white, as is usual in hole-nesting birds. Egg shape varies according to species, individual females, and even among eggs in the same clutch. Published sizes for eggs should be used only as an approximate guide, as variation is so great. Most parrot eggs are ovoid (oval with one end more pointed than the other). The purpose of this shape is that when the narrow ends are pointing inwards, the eggs are more compact, thus minimizing heat loss by reducing the area that the incubating bird has to cover.

The components of the egg are the yolk (that provides the nutrition for the growing embryo), the albumen or egg white (an albuminous sac and liquid albumen, which protect the yolk), the germinal spot from which the embryo will develop, and the membranes. There are two layers of the latter, separated at the blunt end to form an air space. Before hatching, the chick ruptures this membrane with its egg tooth and breathes in the air. The function of the air space is to conserve the limited water supply of the embryo by recondensing respiratory moisture.

The outer layer of the egg is the shell, which consists of about 94% calcium carbonate. It can thus be seen why calcium is vital in the diet of breeding females. The shell is

Enicognathus CONURES

This genus of South American parakeets contains two species: the Slender-billed Conure (*E. leptorhynchus*) and the Austral Conure (*E. ferruginea*). The former is unmistakable because it possesses a very long narrow beak.

Both species have long tails and green plumage, most of the feathers being margined with black or dusky-gray. The forehead and lores are brownish-red (the feathers having a slightly dense, bushy appearance in the Slender-billed Conure). There are some maroon feathers, or a maroon patch on the abdomen.

The length is about 35 cm (14 in) in *E. ferruginea* and about 31 cm (12 in) in the sub-species *minor*, the one usually seen in captivity.

The Slender-billed Conure is a larger bird, of about 41 cm (16 in); the tail accounts for about 17 cm (7 in) of this length. Young Slender-bills have the beak shorter and the bare skin surrounding the eye white (it is gray in adults).

The Austral Conure is not a tropical species, like most other parrots; indeed, it has the most southerly distribution of any member of the family, being found in Tierra del Fuego in Chile, and ranging as far north as southwestern Argentina. Not surprisingly, the plumage of this species is dense. This thick

A parent-reared Slender-billed Conure (*Enicognathus leptorhynchus*), aged 34 days, weighing 284 g (10 oz). The long bill of the adult is not yet apparent.

feathering is utilized in display, when the feathers of the head are puffed out to make the bird look larger than it is.

This conure occurs in forested areas and is associated with *Nothofagus* beech trees. This bird usually nests in hollows in the trees, but one ornithologist has recorded that if such holes are not available, a nest will be built, using twigs or grass stems, among the foliage of the bamboolike *Chusquea*.

Four to eight eggs are laid, and the incubation period is about 25 days.

This species seems to be naturally tame and inquisitive. My own birds delight in nipping fingers at feeding time. One proved amazingly obedient. When I called him he would fly to my shoulder to be returned to his cage. Once inside he would roll over to be tickled, something few parrots permit, yet he would never allow me to scratch his head.

My birds are passionately fond of the strong-tasting buds of lombardy poplar. When bunches are placed in the aviary, they spend hours eating the buds and stripping the bark.

The Slender-billed Conure is found in Chile, where it is declining because of the clearing of forest, excessive hunting, and, apparently, in recent years, Newcastle disease. This species feeds on the ground (on roots), as well as in trees, on

seeds and nuts (especially seeds from the cones of the pine *Araucaria araucana*).

Slender-bills are not popular with farmers, because of their habit of attacking cultivated crops, such as apples. Anyone who has seen a conure tear an apple apart to reach the pips, cannot doubt the damage these birds could cause. After cutting up apples I always give any loose pips to Slender-bills and Australs. After having done this for years I have now read that apple pips are poisonous! It would be interesting to know on what evidence this statement was based.

Slender-bills will breed when only two years old. A female in my possession laid fertile eggs only 18 days after the male was introduced; the clutch consisted of five eggs. Newly hatched chicks weigh about 11 g ($\frac{1}{3}$ oz). Like most conures, Slender-bills are excellent parents and feed enormous amounts to their young. Weight gains of a parent-reared chick were as follows:

day 4, 20 g ($\frac{3}{4}$ oz);
day 10, 57 g (2 oz);
day 11, 78 g ($2\frac{1}{2}$ oz) (eyes open),
day 12, 92 g (3 oz) (ears open),
day 14, 106 g ($3\frac{1}{2}$ oz);
day 16, 130 g ($4\frac{1}{2}$ oz);
day 18, 152 g (5 oz);
day 24, 220 g ($7\frac{1}{2}$ oz) (adult weight).

Rearing foods consisted of sprouted mung beans, sweet corn

(thawed frozen kernels; whole fresh corn on the cob would have been better if available), wholegrain bread and milk with a powdered calcium and Vitamin D3 supplement, and soaked sunflower seed. Smaller quantities of celery, peas, and apple were taken. When blackberries ripened, these were consumed with great eagerness. Slender-bills are also passionately fond of hawthorn berries. The young leave the nest at about seven and a half weeks old.

Owners of this species should note that they must have a deep container for drinking water; they have an unusual method of drinking that involves tipping the head right back.

Eolophus COCKATOO – see under *COCKATOOS*

Eos LORIES

Members of this genus are predominantly red, and small to medium in size – 23–31 cm (9–12 in). The bill is orange. These lories occur on various islands of New Guinea and Indonesia. The best known is undoubtedly the Red Lory (*Eos bornea*), which is almost entirely red, with some blue and black on the wings and undertail coverts. Free-breeding and beautiful, it is an ideal species for beginners with lories. However, it is prone to feather plucking and to plucking its young.

The diet is similar to that described for the *Chalcopsitta* lories, but members of this genus are more willing to try a variety of items, including green food.

As with all *Eos* species, two eggs are laid and incubated for about 24 days by the female. The young spend nine weeks or more in the nest. Immature birds have many feathers with dark tips, thus giving a mottled appearance.

The least typical member of the genus is the beautiful Blue-streaked Lory (*E. reticulata*) from the Tenimber Islands in Indonesia, where its numbers must now have declined after severe deforestation in the area. This lory has a longer tail than other *Eos*, and also pronounced blue shaft-streaked feathers on the neck; if it had bare skin surrounding the lower mandible it would surely have been classified as a *Chalcopsitta*.

Probably the most free-breeding member of the genus is the smallest species, the Violet-necked or Violet-naped Lory (*E. squamata*) from the western Papuan Islands. Its red plumage is irregularly marked with dull purple on the abdomen and neck. Some pairs are continuous breeders and will produce eight or more young a year if the chicks are removed for hand-rearing at an early age. This becomes essential if they are severely plucked, as so often happens.

Eunymphicus PARAKEETS

The two beautiful and unusual crested parakeets that form this genus are generally considered as subspecies. In the opinion of one of perhaps only three or four aviculturists, who has extensive experience of both birds, they should be classified as separate species.

Their plumage differs little, apart from head coloration. The Horned Parakeet (*E. cornutus cornutus*) is the more colorful, with its bright red forehead and crown, and yellow on its nape. The Uvaean Parakeet (*E. c. uvaeensis*) lacks the yellow, and also the red tip to the crest feathers, and has only a small area of red on the forehead. Its beak is noticeably larger. The orange-red iris is striking in both birds, partly because of the contrast with the jet black feathers surrounding it.

In young birds the face is grayish, not black, and this area is reduced. The feathers of the forehead are black tipped with red. In the Horned Parakeet, the ear coverts are pale green instead of yellow. The bill is horn-colored and the iris is brownish.

The Horned Parakeet is found on the volcanic island of New Caledonia in the western Pacific. This forms an area of about 18,650 sq km (7,200 sq miles). The stronghold of this species is the Haute Yate Reserve – but it has declined there because of the destruction of its habitat.

In contrast, the Uvaean Parakeet occurs only on Ouvea, one of the Loyalty Islands, a dependency of New Caledonia. Because of its tiny area of distribution, this is one of the most vulnerable of all parrots. Its range is only 4 or 5 km (2½–3 miles) in extent. Among parrots, only the Cayman Brac Amazon (*Amazona leucocephala hesterna*) has a similarly small area of distribution.

The population of *uvaeensis* is believed to number in the region of 200, having declined because of deforestation and the further destruction of the forests by fire.

The *Eunymphicus* are intriguing birds – beautiful, intelligent, and very quick on the wing. Loro Parque is probably the only place where both species can be seen side by side; here a pair of Horned Parakeets are housed next to two male Uvaean. The latter are more timid, generally retreating to the depth of their 9 m (29½ ft) long aviary, whereas the Horned Parakeets are tamer and more inquisitive. Both are strong and agile in flight.

Horned Parakeets have been bred since the 1970s in a few collections in Germany and Switzerland, and in one collection in France. Three or four eggs are laid and incubated for about 22 days. The young spend five or six weeks in the nest. These birds have a marked need for animal protein when rearing young, and will consume mealworms, meat, and cheese.

This species remains rare and expensive, but is gradually being established.

EXHIBITING
All shows for cage birds of every type have classes for parrots and other members of the parrot family. Generally, however, these shows are not well supported. Those who keep parrots in aviaries are seldom prepared to move them to a show hall, especially as shows are normally staged at the coldest time of the year. The species seen at shows are generally those kept by fanciers, i.e., people who breed for show or color; likely exhibits are lovebirds, cockatiels, and Grass Parakeets (*Neophemas*) mainly, plus the pet parrots of the club members.

It is permitted to exhibit large parrots in the cages in which they are kept, whereas others must be staged in proper show cages. Although there are no standard sizes, the cages must conform to the usual pattern and be painted white inside and black outside.

The prospective exhibitor should be familiar with the way the birds are staged and should visit a show or consult an experienced exhibitor. Enough food should be placed in the cage to last for the duration of the show. Special items, such as spray millet or fruit, can be given by the exhibitor *after* judging.

What does the judge look for? Primarily, perfect feather condition, but the bird must show itself well for this to be evident. It

must be steady and at ease in the cage. Rarity of species should be considered only after these points have been taken into account.

Some of the larger shows have classes for talking birds, in which case the entries are judged solely on their talking ability. This class can draw the largest crowd, as people love to be entertained by talking birds.

Talented mimics such as Gray Parrots are a great attraction at shows that include classes for talkers.

F

FEATHER

Several different types of feathers are found in parrots. All birds have *contour feathers*, that is, the external feathers with naked, tapering bases of the shafts (quills or calami); which, in parrots, are so much admired for their colors. In parrots these grow from tracts of skin (called pterylae): the areas between these (apteria) are actually bare. This is not apparent unless one parts the feathers, because all areas are covered by overlapping feathers. One can, for example, part the feathers on an Amazon's neck to reveal comparatively large bare areas.

The feather tracts have different arrangements in different species. These can be seen most easily in chicks just before the feathers start to erupt.

Parrots also possess *down feathers*, or plumules, which have little or no quill and grow from the skin of all parts of the body except the neck. These have a fluffy texture, and are not tightly knit like the contour feathers. The color of down varies in different species, but is usually white, pale yellow, or gray. In some Amazons, the newly opened down feathers are yellow, but soon fade to white.

Density of down also varies; species from high altitudes naturally have denser down than lowland birds. In chicks there are two kinds of down: the *natal down* (of newly hatched chicks), which is a very simple type, and the *second down*, which appears in most parrot species at between about 10 and 20 days.

A third type of special modified feather is the *powder down* – a down feather that is believed to grow throughout the life of the bird. The barbs of this feather disintegrate to produce a fine powder that is used for cleaning the feathers. This is more evident in some species than in others. Cockatoos, for example, give off clouds of dust from their powder down feathers; this should be borne in mind by anyone with allergies or chest complaints. The dust will be less of a nuisance in a pet bird if it is sprayed daily with warm water.

A few parrots also have *bristles* or filoplumes (more commonly found in softbill species, such as barbets, and also in pigeons). These are actually contour feathers that lack the barbs (the fine filaments attached to the central shaft). Bristles, which are very sensitive to vibration and pressure, were apparent around the eyes and cere of a young Lesser Vasa Parrot (hand-reared and therefore tolerant of close examination). The eyelashes of parrots (more prominent in some species than others) are the same type of feather.

The range of colors found in members of the parrot family is surely more diverse than in any other group of birds. Plumage coloration and markings are extremely varied within the different genera. They could be placed in categories according to the continent from which they originate. Given a single parrot feather, someone with a good knowledge of parrots could tell you whether the owner of that feather originated from South America or from Australia, for example, even if that expert could not name the species.

In parrot feathers, there are two types of colors: structural and pigmentary. A feather consists of a central shaft to which the barbs are attached. Each barb has two rows of side branches, the *barbules*. The components responsible for structural color are present in the barbs and barbules. Some colors are due principally to the back-scattering of light from the many hollow keratin cylinders that make up the spongy structure of the barbs. Iridescent colors are believed to result from barbules that are flattened for part of their length and twisted at right angles.

The other factor responsible for feather color is pigment. There are a number of types of pigment, the most common of which is melanin; while another type is carotenoid. There are also other pigments of unknown composition. Color in parrot feathers can also be the result of the combination of pigmentary and structural colors.

A wonderful range of colors may

A pair of
Citron-crested
Cockatoos *(Cacatua
sulphurea
citrinocristata)*. The
difference in eye
color between males
and females is
obvious.

Cockatoos (2)

A captive-bred Banksian Cockatoo, or Red-tailed Black Cockatoo *(Calyptorhynchus magnificus)*.

Leadbeater's Cockatoo *(Cacatua leadbeateri)* – usually considered the most beautiful of the white cockatoos.

be found in one feather. In the feathers of neotropical species, for example, the upper and lower surface of the feather has different coloration. In some feathers, the manner in which one color fades into another is remarkably subtle; in others the colors are sharply divided.

FEATHER PLUCKING

Nearly all cases of self feather mutilation are due to some form of stress. This includes the unfulfilled desire to breed that is so common in parrots kept singly. As soon as the problem becomes evident, it is important to try to find the cause. In some cases, notably Gray Parrots, it can be so severe and so rapid that the main hope of curing the problem, i.e., pairing the bird for breeding, is ruled out because a badly plucked bird cannot be kept out of doors, behave normally, or incubate efficiently.

Certain parrots of a nervous temperament are very prone to the problem: Queen of Bavaria's Conures, Red-fronted Macaws, and Gang Gang Cockatoos are notorious. Keeping them supplied daily with fresh branches may help. Sometimes they regrow all their feathers and look superb – then, in a couple of hours, they denude

themselves completely again, in response to some form of stress. Some pet Gray Parrots, for example, are so easily stressed that this behavior can be caused by any alteration to the cage or its position.

Feather plucking is rarely the result of incorrect feeding or feather mites, as is sometimes suggested. It could be caused by irritated dry skin, however, and this is one reason why regular spraying is so important.

Many cases of plucking first occur when a single bird reaches sexual maturity – an indication that it needs a mate. However, many birds, such as lovebirds and cockatiels, will also pluck their mates or their young. On removing the young birds when they are independent, the feathers usually grow in a few weeks.

All in all, feather plucking is usually a difficult problem to deal with; one has to try to understand the psychology of the bird in order to rectify the cause where self-plucking is concerned.

FERAL PARROTS

Feral populations are those that establish themselves outside their native habitat. They are derived from escaped or released cage birds. Certain species are remarkable for their ability to thrive in almost any habitat and, with a little help in the way of food, any climate. The Indian Ringneck Parakeet, for example, can be found in small groups in several areas of England, aided by winter feeding. A few breeding successes may occur, but the groups have always remained small.

On the other hand, in more favorable climates the species can multiply to the degree that it becomes an agricultural pest. It may even occupy the niche once held by an extinct species or a species that is extinct in the area. In Puerto Rico, for example, where the native parrot is now confined to the Luquillo Mountains, the Hispaniolan Amazon (from the neighboring island on which Haiti and Santo Domingo are located) is fairly well established in the lowlands. Other smaller parrots, such as *Aratinga* conures from South America, are also breeding there.

Feather plucking is very common in Gray Parrots (*Psittacus erithacus erithacus*). It usually begins with the removal of a few feathers from the breast.

An introduced species can pose a very serious threat to an endangered species. On the island of Mauritius in the Indian Ocean the introduced Indian Ringneck could become a nest competitor against the critically endangered Echo Parakeet (*Psittacula eques*), of which only about a dozen are known to survive.

Feral species are usually those which are already widespread and numerous in their country of origin because they are able to adapt to a wide variety of habitats. This is true of the Ringneck Parakeet. Or they may have established themselves because their adopted country has many similarities to their native country.

In South Florida there are thriving feral populations of parrots and parakeets from South America (also mynahs from Asia). In December, 1987 I visited the roosting site of one such flock. Located a few feet from a busy road, the site was a small stand of casuarina trees by an apartment building. Across the street was a park containing plenty of trees, making one wonder why this particular stand was so attractive to the parrots.

FIG PARROTS (*Opopsitta* and *Psittaculirostris*)

The small and extremely beautiful Fig Parrots are difficult subjects in captivity. Very rarely imported until the early 1970s, much remains to be learned about them, as captive breeding has succeeded only rarely. Active, quiet, and fascinating to observe, they are among the most attractive aviary birds imaginable.

The *Psittaculirostris* species originate from New Guinea. They measure about 18 cm (7 in). The smaller *Opopsitta* is 13–14 cm (about 5 in) and is found in New Guinea, Australia, and the Aru Islands of Indonesia.

Sexual dimorphism is marked or absent. All have large heads, strong bills, and very short pointed tails.

The diet must contain large quantities of fruit, including dried figs that should be soaked in water overnight. Each bird should be offered daily at least three figs – more if small ones are used. A Vitamin K supplement (either drops or crushed tablets) should be added to the figs two or three times a week. Without this vitamin, laying females may hemorrhage, and other distressing problems may occur.

Apple, pear, grapes, and cactus fruits are relished; some Fig Parrots will also eat banana and pomegranate. A seed mixture containing sunflower seeds and various smaller seeds should always be available; spray millet is relished.

Fresh branches for gnawing are essential if the beak is not to become overgrown. If suitable branches are not available, the

aviary woodwork and perches will be attacked. Like lories, these birds need a nest box to retire to when night falls or when danger threatens.

There are two species of *Opopsitta*, the Double-eyed (*O. diophthalma*), which is rare in captivity, and the Orange-breasted (*O. gulielmiterti*), which is extremely rare. The Double-eyed Parrot is green, with the forehead red and a touch of sky blue above the eye. The cheeks are red in the male and whitish in the female. This species is difficult to establish when newly imported; even acclimatized birds should not be subjected to temperatures lower than 10°C (50°F).

The clutch consists of two eggs that are incubated for 18 to 20 days. In one carefully documented record of captive breeding, a young bird left the nest at 52 days; in another, the single youngster spent about 39 days in the nest.

The three species of *Psittaculirostris* are among my own favorite parrots. Salvadori's (*P. salvadorii*) has the feathers of its cheeks (yellow in the male and greenish-yellow in the female) elongated and standing away from

Orange-breasted Fig Parrots of two different sub-species: *Opopsitta gulielmi nigrifons* and, second from right, *O.g. amabilis.*

Cockatoos (3)

The Philippine Cockatoo, or Red-vented Cockatoo *(Cacatua haematuropygia)* is not frequently available.

A Palm Cockatoo *(Probosciger aterrimus)* – a magnificent bird from New Guinea.

55

The White-tailed
Black Cockatoo
(*Calyptorhynchus
funereus baudinii*) is
rare in captivity and
declining in the wild.

the head. The male has the upper breast red, this area being bluish-green in the female.

Desmarest's (*P. desmarestii*) is an extremely beautiful bird with a scarlet forehead and golden-orange on the crown and nape; below the eye is a small patch of brilliant blue. The area below the throat is sky blue and wine-colored in the Desmarest's Fig Parrot, in which male and female are alike.

In the subspecies *godmani*, the male has the hind-neck yellow; the female lacks this.

Edwards's (*P. edwardsii*) is easily distinguished by its dark red cheeks, the feathers of which are elongated, as are those of the bright yellow ear coverts. In the male the breast is dark red, in the female it is yellow-green.

Any breeding success can be classed as an achievement. I believe that a diet that includes animal protein, such as mealworms, greatly increases the chance of a chick being reared. A Salvadori's hatched at Loro Parque thrived until the age of six weeks, when, sadly, it died of enteritis: for the first three or four weeks the parents consumed at least 100 mealworms daily. (In hot weather it is impossible to keep and feed them because they are attacked by ants.) In later clutches, when mealworms were not available, chicks, which hatched on three occasions, survived less than a week.

These Fig Parrots lay two eggs, which are incubated by the female for about 24 days. The young leave the nest after eight weeks. They can be kept in colonies.

FOOT
There are several different toe formations in birds, that of parrots being zygodactyl, that is, two toes point forwards and two point backwards. The curved claws provide a strong grip and the toenails are quite sharp in the larger species (agonizingly so in the very young of some birds, such as Gray Parrots). The foot is covered in scales, reminiscent of snake skin. This skin is probably molted once a year (certainly the case in my pet Yellow-fronted Amazon).

Many genera of parrots (such as *Amazona*, *Cacatua*, *Calyptorhynchus*, and *Poicephalus*) use a foot to hold food; it is a very efficient grasping tool. Some (such as *Ara* and *Amazona*) also use the foot in defense when perched; in the nest they will turn over on their backs and strike upwards with the feet (*Ara*). Nestlings will do this instinctively. Many parrots, especially those mentioned above, use a foot to scratch their heads.

FORCE-FEEDING
At times force-feeding is essential to save the life of a bird. It may cease to feed itself because it is sick or severely stressed, or because it is a recently captured wild bird. Force-feeding may also be necessary to ensure that a bird is receiving sufficient food, or more nutritious food than that which it chooses. Most young birds can be spoon-fed unless removed from the nest near to the age of fledging when they are too big (see *GRIT*).

Force-feeding is accomplished with the aid of a syringe. Most pharmacies sell plastic disposable syringes that are ideal for the purpose after the needle has been discarded. A length of plastic tubing, of a suitable size for the bird concerned, is attached to the syringe. The food used could consist of high protein baby cereal, a vitamin and mineral supplement, and Ringer's lactate (a physiological solution containing various salts and minerals, obtainable from a veterinarian), or water, preferably distilled or non-carbonated mineral water.

The toe formation in parrots is zygodactyl; that is, two toes point forward and two backward.

The food must be of a consistency to flow through the syringe. Additional items to those suggested must be blended very well to avoid the frustration of a syringe blocked by a small fragment of food.

The syringe should be prepared by lubricating the leading edge of the inner part (the plunger) with petroleum jelly to ensure its moving freely. When filled, the syringe should be turned upside down and the plunger should be depressed a little to expel any air. The plastic tube should be dipped into hot water before being placed in the bird's mouth, to ensure that it is warm and slides easily into the crop. The food must, of course, also have been warmed, then stirred well to eliminate hot spots.

The tube should be inserted down the right side of the bird's throat. The syringe is then slowly compressed to release the food. With a large and powerful parrot, such as a macaw, it is advisable for two people to carry out the task of force-feeding. One holds the bird steady and also holds the joint of the plastic tube to the syringe. The force of the pumping action could result in the tube's losing contact with the syringe and the bird's swallowing of the tube.

Great care must be taken to ensure that the tube enters the crop, which it is almost certain to do if directed to the right side of the throat. If food were to enter the lungs, the bird would drown instantly.

***Forpus* PARROTLETS** – see *PARROTLETS* (*Forpus*)

FRACTURES
If your bird breaks a leg or a wing, do not panic. You will need to seek the advice of an avian veterinarian who is used to handling pet birds, but in the meantime keep the patient warm, using a heat lamp if necessary. Keep the bird as inactive as possible. A glass-fronted aquarium or brooder is ideal for this purpose, because the bird is unable to climb about. As a temporary measure, a cardboard box will suffice for smaller birds.

A veterinarian can advise one of three courses of action: surgery, fixing the limb externally (by means of a splint, for example), or simply trying to keep the bird as inactive as possible.

There are several factors to be considered. Not all vets have the necessary experience with birds to operate on them. Surgery is usually more expensive, but healing is generally more rapid than with other methods. Surgery is not usually practicable for small birds.

Not all birds will tolerate a splint; a neck brace may have to be put on the bird to prevent its removing the splint – and this could be the cause of more stress. One danger of a splint is that the bandage holding it in place may be applied so tight, that the blood supply to the limb is cut off. The patient then loses all sensation in that area and may bite off the limb. This is what happened to a Jendaya Conure whose leg splint was bound too tightly. After three or four days it chewed its leg off. (Fortunately, it was young and quickly adapted to its disability.)

It may be necessary to delay treatment for a bird suffering from shock, until it has recovered from the initial stress. On the other hand, many cases of broken legs need urgent attention.

In an emergency a leg splint can be made from a small plastic syringe cut in half lengthwise, or from a piece of lightweight aluminum shaped to the leg. Absorbent cotton should be placed between the splint and the tape used to bind it to the leg. A broken wing can also be taped to the body – but not so tightly that it constricts the chest, which could result in suffocation. However, broken limbs should always be attended to by a veterinarian, who may have the facilities to x-ray the patient. This will reveal whether the bone is infected – a serious condition known as osteomyelitis. Since some bones communicate with the air sacs, infections can result from external contamination.

Chicks with fractures can be treated in the same way. Splints and bandages can be very stressful to chicks at first, although they generally tolerate them quite well after a while. A broken leg can be mended perfectly after two weeks. During this period the diet should include a calcium/Vitamin D3 supplement. Chicks suffering from rickets, due to lack of calcium, are a tragic sight, possibly with several

Lories (1)

The Tahiti Blue Lory *(Vini peruviana),* found on a few small islands of the Pacific, is declining in the wild and an extreme rarity in captivity.

The most readily available of the *Lorius* lories, the Chattering *(Lorius garrulus garrulus),* is a delightful aviary bird.

The Yellow-streaked
Lory *(Chalcopsitta
scintillata)*.

fractures of the leg and/or wings. Usually there is no option but to destroy these chicks – a sad waste of young life and a distressing experience that could so easily have been avoided.

FRENCH MOLT
This is the term given to malformation and loss of the flight and tail feathers in birds in nest feather. The degree of severity varies; in some cases the feathers are replaced by normal ones, but in many instances the replacement feathers soon drop out or are poorly formed, with blood remaining in the quill. In severe cases the bird is never able to fly. French molt is best known, and has been extensively studied, in budgerigars, but it could occur in any psittacine species. It is not confined solely to birds in captivity, but has been recorded in the wild in a number of species of Australian parrots.

There are numerous theories regarding the cause of French molt, none of which has been proved conclusively. However, it seems likely that a number of factors are to blame. A virus is most likely, especially papovavirus, also known as budgerigar fledgling disease.

It should be noted that in

Missing tail and flight feathers indicate that this young budgerigar is suffering from French molt.

Australia, the term French molt is used for psittacine beak and feather disease (*PB* and *FDS*).

FRUITS
Newcomers to keeping parrots are often cautious in their choice of fruits; they may even withhold fruit totally because it makes their parrot's feces loose. However, loose droppings are only a cause for concern when the diet consists almost entirely of hard seeds (highly unnatural), not when it contains soft items on a daily basis.

Fruit should not be rationed. Few species, except those that require large amounts, such as Hawk-headed Parrots and caiques, will eat excessive quantities.

It is difficult to persuade many wild-caught imported parrots to eat fruit. Perseverance over a long period may be necessary. Where possible, a bird that refuses fruit should be kept near, or with one which relishes it.

Apples   These are perhaps the most widely fed fruits and among the most popular. However, there are over 2,000 varieties, not all of which are eaten with equal relish. Apples can be fed cut into slices; for small species half an apple can be spiked onto a nail on the perch.

Apricots   These would be an excellent food for parrots if one could persuade them to eat this fruit. They retain their high Vitamin A content even when cooked, dried, or canned, and many parrots suffer diseases because their diet is deficient in Vitamin A. The carotene content of apricots is also very high.

Avocado   is poisonous to parrots. Do not feed it.

Bananas   The liking for this fruit appears to be very much an individual taste where parrots are concerned. Some lories and macaws will eat large quantities, but parakeets ignore this fruit.

Blackberry (*Rubus fruticosus*)   The European blackberry is relished by some parrots and ignored by others.

Cherry (sweet)   This is a great favorite of many of the larger species, especially those with a bill strong enough to crack the pit, which is apparently considered a great delicacy. The flesh may be eaten or discarded in the haste to reach the stone. It should be noted that the leaves of the wild cherry are said to be poisonous.

Elderberry (*Sambucus* genus)   The berries are an excellent food for parrots, enjoyed by many species. During an autumn when elderberries are plentiful, it is worth freezing some. Fresh berries contain a small quantity of the amino acid tyrosin.

Fig   This is a natural food for many species. However, expensive fresh figs were untouched by my parrots, whereas dried figs, which have been soaked in water overnight, are highly favored by certain species. Fig Parrots (*Psittaculirostris* and *Opopsitta*) should receive at least two daily.

Grapes   Table grapes are relished by all the larger parrots and by some of the small ones. Some birds will discard the fruit to reach the pips, which are highly favored.

Kiwi   An excellent food if parrots will eat it. The content of potassium, calcium, magnesium and Vitamin C is high.

Mango   Juicy and fleshy when ripe, a mango is difficult to cut. Where it is grown locally, it is worth feeding; imported mangoes are expensive. Their nutritional value is high: mangoes contain large amounts of carotene, minerals (including potassium), and Vitamin C.

Nectarine   This mutant of the peach, which has firmer flesh, is a good food for any parrot that will eat it, being a fine source of carotene and potassium.

Orange   Many parrots, especially lories and the larger South American species, relish oranges. Generally, the best way to feed an orange is to leave the skin intact and to cut the orange into pieces, or into halves for lories and other birds that like to dig into fruit. Usually the rough-skinned varieties are preferred to those with smooth skins. Juicy mandarins, clementines, and tangerines are also enjoyed. Some oranges are treated with fungicides and pesticides, so the skins should be scrubbed in warm water to remove these. This is especially important for those birds which chew up, and probably eat, some of the skin.

Palm Fruits   Many parrots enjoy the fruits of palm trees, such as those of the Queen's Palm (*Arecastrum romanzoffianum*). At Loro Parque in Tenerife, the Canary Islands, where this palm grows freely, species as small as parrotlets (*Forpus*) and as large as macaws, relish palm fruits. Amazons and the larger *Psittacula* parakeets are especially fond of them. The fruits are orange, round, and about 2.5 cm (1 in) long, with a fibrous exterior and a very hard stone inside .

A Pesquet's Parrot (*Psittrichas fulgidus*) scooping out the flesh from an apple.

Lories (2)

Black Lories
(Chalcopsitta atra)
from New Guinea –
not a colorful
species, but
intelligent and
vivacious.

A Dusky Lory
(Pseudeos fuscata) at
Loro Parque,
Tenerife.

Lorikeets

One of the many subspecies of the Green-naped Lorikeet, Mitchell's Lorikeet *(Trichoglossus haematodus mitchellii)*, is distinguished by its red breast.

Josephine's Lorikeet *(Charmosyna josefinae)* male (right) with youngster, at Loro Parque, in Tenerife, Canary Islands.

Male (left) and female Red-flanked Lorikeets *(Charmosyna placentis)* could be mistaken for different species.

G

Papaya   Unripe papaya contains the protein-splitting enzyme papain, which is highly efficient in aiding digestion. Ripe papaya contains only a small amount of papain, but is still a useful aid to digestion. Papaya is a valuable addition to any formula used for hand-rearing chicks, but especially for chicks that are not digesting their food well. Papaya should also be given to any parrot suffering from a pancreatic disorder.

Peach   This fruit is easily digested, contains vitamins and minerals, and is extremely rich in carotene. However, not many parrots will eat it. For years I gave peach stones to the larger parrots in my collection, because they relish the almond-like nut in the stone, until I learned that this nut contains poisonous prussic acid.

Pear   This will be eaten only at the correct stage of ripeness; overripe fruits are always ignored. Pears should be juicy, not hard, and certainly not mushy.

Plum   A good food if acceptable; plums contain carotene, calcium, and potassium.

Pomegranate   This fruit is favored more highly than any other by the majority of parrots. Nutritionally excellent, it is expensive, and availability is normally limited to a period of about three months. Because of its price, it is likely to be fed in moderation. Some birds would eat little else, given the opportunity, and when the season ends this could be a problem.

Prickly pear   Where it is available this is an excellent food.

Raspberry   This fruit is excellent nutritionally, but favored by very few parrots, and usually these consume only the pips. The potassium content is high, and there are smaller amounts of calcium, magnesium, iron, carotene, and the B vitamins.

Strawberry   The vitamin and mineral content of this fruit is high, but very few parrots will sample it.

GANG GANG COCKATOO
(*Callocephalon fimbriatum*)
The only member of its genus, this species is nearer the Black Cockatoos in appearance and behavior, but is much smaller – only 35 cm (13½ in). Unmistakable, it is mainly gray with lighter gray and white margins to most of the feathers; the male has a red head; the female's crest and head are gray. Young birds can be sexed as soon as they feather, because the immature cocks have crests tipped with red.

Originating from Australia, this cockatoo is rare in captivity outside that country. Of a nervous disposition and extremely susceptible to feather plucking, it should be provided with fresh-cut branches daily, and also pine cones.

The diet should include few sunflower seeds, but plenty of small seeds (to keep the birds occupied), hulled oats, canary grass seed, chicken bones, berries, such as hawthorn (eaten in the wild), a considerable amount of nuts (peanuts, almonds, and walnuts), fruit (pear, apple, pomegranates, grapes), greens, and just a few mealworms. This species is quite unsuitable for a cage.

The clutch consists of two eggs, incubated by male and female for 28 days. The young spend approximately seven weeks in the nest but are fed by both parents for an additional month.

Geoffroyus PARROTS
This genus of parrots, from Indonesia, New Guinea, and the northern tip of Australia (Cape York), is never likely to be known to aviculturists. There are records of only five birds being kept outside their country of origin, none of which survived more than a few months. One of them was recorded as eating seeds and fruit, so diet was not the problem.

There are three species, none of which appears to be rare in the wild. They are secretive birds and little is known of their natural history.

The Red-cheeked Parrot (*G. geoffroyi*), which has many subspecies almost throughout the entire range of the genus, is the most beautiful. The coloration, like the bird, is very delicate. The male's head is rose-red and pale mauve – a particularly lovely combination. The plumage is otherwise green, except for reddish-brown on the wing coverts and blue underwing coverts. The female differs in having her head and nape brown and her beak dusky olive. Young birds have the head green, the cheeks and throat being tinged with brown. In length this bird is about 21 cm (8½ in).

Geopsittacus – see *NIGHT PARROT*

GLAUCOUS MACAW – see under *HYACINTHINE MACAW*

Glossopsitta LORIKEETS

The three small lorikeets in this genus are virtually unknown outside Australia.

Extremely attractive aviary birds, they differ from other lorikeets in laying larger clutches (three to five eggs) and in the shorter period the young spend in the nest, as short as 40 days in the Little Lorikeet (*G. pusilla*).

This species measures only 15 cm (6 in). Mainly green, the face is red (duller in the female) and the beak is black.

The equally small Purple-crowned Lorikeet (*G. porphyrocephala*) is a little gem that aviculturists outside Australia would love to obtain. Friendly and inquisitive, it can be bred on the colony system. Beautifully marked, its forehead and ear coverts are yellow and orange, its crown purple, and its underparts bright blue, with a yellow patch on the side of the breast. The bill is black.

The Musk Lorikeet (*G. concinna*) is currently kept in two or three zoos outside Australia. Measuring 23 cm (10 in), the forehead and a large patch behind the eye are red; there is a patch of golden-brown on the mantle, and yellow on the side of the breast. This species requires a varied diet that includes plenty of seed.

GRASS PARAKEETS (*Neophema*)

Small and immensely popular, the vividly colored Grass Parakeets have long been favorites with beginners. Breeding results are usually good. These birds originate from Australia, and five of the seven species are well known in aviculture. One, the migratory and very sociable Orange-bellied (*N. chrysogaster*), is one of the most endangered birds in Australia.

Measuring 19–23 cm (7½–9 in), they need only small enclosures of 1.8–2.4 m (6–8 ft) long, 76 cm (30 in) wide and 1.8 m (6 ft) high. Enclosed winter accommodation, of either a shelter or entrance to a bird room, is recommended in colder climates, because Grass Parakeets do not tolerate cold damp weather well. Suspended aviaries are not recommended, as *Neophemas* like to walk about on the floor. Grass floors are seldom practical, but growing grass from seed in boxes and placing the boxes in the aviaries will provide these parakeets much enjoyment.

The diet should be as recommended for cockatiels.

Breeding usually commences at one year old, when Grass Parakeets should be provided with a nest box measuring 15 cm (6 in) square and about 31 cm (12 in) high. Four to six eggs, and occasionally more, form the clutch, and the incubation period is about 19 days. The female might not commence to incubate until the second or third egg has been laid. The young usually remain in the nest for 28 to 30 days, sometimes less.

In an aviary longer than 1.8 m (6 ft), precautions must be taken to prevent the birds killing or injuring themselves by flying into the wire when they leave the nest. Consider this in advance and grow a shrub, such as honeysuckle or even morning glory, over the end of the aviary, and place plenty of branches inside, or even tie strips of white material to the wire.

One of the most brilliantly colored birds in existence, the male Splendid Parakeet (*N. splendida*) or Scarlet-chested Parakeet must be responsible for attracting many people to parakeet breeding. The head, shoulders, and edge of the wing are blue, the breast is scarlet, and the abdomen and underside of the tail are yellow; the rest of the plumage is green. In females and young birds the underparts are

A pair of Bourke's Parakeets.

entirely yellow, and the blue in the plumage is less extensive and duller. (The shade of blue is lighter than that of the female Turquoisine.)

A gentle bird, the Splendid can be kept with finches, but not with other parakeets. In general, *Neophema* species should be housed as one pair per aviary and definitely not with other members of their own genus.

The male of Turquoisine (*N. pulchella*) has a dark red bar down the wing; the underparts are entirely yellow, except for an orange patch on the abdomen. Some breeders pair birds together to accentuate this feature and call the resulting young "Orange-bellied" Turquoisines.

The female has less blue on the face than the male, lacks the red in the wing and has a breast of dull green. Immature birds are more like the female, but males often have a little red in the wing and more blue on their faces than do young females.

Two species liable to cause confusion are the Elegant (*N. elegans*) and the Blue-winged (*N. chrysostoma*) Grass Parakeets. Both have a dark blue band on the forehead, edged with lighter blue, and bright yellow lores. They are olive green above and on the upper breast, with yellow underparts; some birds also have a touch of orange on the abdomen. The main difference lies in the wings: in the Blue-winged Grass Parakeet the wing coverts are deeper blue and this area is more extensive than in

the Elegant Grass Parakeet, which has most of the wing coverts green, not blue. The Elegant is a yellower shade of green, and the light blue following the dark blue on the forehead is much brighter. In the Blue-winged, the primaries are jet black in the male and brownish-black in the female. Females are duller than males and immature birds are duller than females.

Unmistakable in its coloration, Bourke's Parakeet (*N. bourkii*) is mainly brown above, with buff margins to the feathers, pinkish-brown below, with pink on the abdomen, and blue on the wings and on the under tail coverts. In the male the forehead is blue.

There is a blue mutation in which the green areas are replaced by blue (the shade varies), the red by pinkish-apricot and the yellow by creamy white.

GRAY PARROT (*Psittacus erithacus*)

The Gray Parrot, famed for its mimicry, is ever in demand. Increasingly the demand is being met by captive-bred birds, but the trade in wild-caught specimens is still substantial. This is to be deplored, because many of these wild-caught parrots are adults that are stressed by capture and by captivity, and their survival rate is not high. There should be restrictions on the export of this species, but it is, of course, a source of much-needed revenue to African countries.

Dealers advertise different

names for this parrot, such as Congo Gray and Silver Gray, but there are only two subspecies. Grays do vary in the depth of gray, according to origin and sex (males normally being darker). The only subspecies known in aviculture, the *timneh* (not *timor*, as some advertisers insist), *P.e. timneh* is distinctive. It is smaller, about 29 cm (11 in) as against approximately 33 cm (13 in) for *P. erithacus*, has a dull red tail, not a scarlet tail, and has part of the upper mandible orange-brown.

P. erithacus inhabits a wide area of western central Africa; *timneh* occurs in Liberia and a small part of the Ivory Coast, Sierra Leone, and southern Guinea. The species is common in some areas, and declining in others with the destruction of its habitat (forested plains, wooded savannas, and, occasionally, mangrove swamps).

Although so popular, it is not necessarily an easy subject in captivity, being very easily stressed (see *STRESS* and *FEATHER PLUCKING*). Many imported birds take years to be persuaded to accept any food but sunflower seed. There is also a high risk of disease in imported birds (even though they have been quarantined for the required period). A captive-bred bird is recommended; it will cost more, but this is negligible in terms of a companion for life. The potential life span of large parrots, such as Grays and Amazons, is 60 years, and possibly more.

Like any other parrot, in order to tame them and teach them to talk, Grays must be acquired when young – that is, while the eye is still gray or grayish-yellow (not clear yellow as in birds of one year and more). Their temperament varies greatly, but most Grays are really friendly only towards their owner or a few people whom they know well. They may exhibit a marked dislike of men or women (not invariably related to their own sex) and many will allow only one person to handle them. Generally, they are not to be trusted with people they do not know, and although they turn their heads invitingly to be scratched, in many cases this is because they are awaiting the opportunity for a sly bite!

The diet should be as

recommended for Amazons, but Grays do not so readily accept a wide variety of foods, unless very tame.

Compatibility is of great importance in breeding Grays. Many pairs never attempt to breed, or possibly consist of two males or two females, although the owner is convinced by their behavior that they are a true pair. Feather or surgical sexing is advisable, unless a Gray has actually laid or fertilized eggs.

The clutch usually consists of three or four eggs (rarely five) and the incubation period is 28 to 30 days. The young spend about 12 weeks in the nest.

Graydidascalus brachyurus – see *SHORT-TAILED PARROT*

GRIT

Do parrots need grit? The answer is that some do and some do not. There are many different factors to take into account. In the wild, seed-eating birds of many species – not only parrots – swallow pieces of grit, shell, or small stones. These end up in the muscular stomach or gizzard (proventriculus) into which food passes after it has left the crop. In the gizzard the food is ground up before the nutrients are assimilated into the body. This is achieved by the food's being rubbed against grit or other small hard items. If such items are not present, hard items of food may leave the bird's body undigested. (Note, however, that undigested particles of food in the feces may have other causes, such as malfunction of the pancreas.)

To assess whether your birds need grit, consider the following factors:
1 Diet – birds such as lories and Hanging Parrots, whose food consists almost entirely of soft items, do not need grit; indeed, the gizzard is poorly developed.
2 Birds kept in outdoor aviaries may be satisfying their need for small hard particles in the gizzard by swallowing pieces of stones from the floor, by gnawing the wall and, I suspect, by swallowing small pieces of wood gnawed from perches or branches. I know of a pair of Hyacinthine Macaws, kept at liberty, that consumed large amounts of limestone, especially

while rearing a chick. Birds kept in cages have no access to such items and should be offered grit at least once a month, although it may be ignored most or even all of the time.

3 Certain species seem to have a greater need for grit than others; for example, most cockatiels and budgerigars consume grit with great enthusiasm. It may be that ground-feeding species need grit the most, because their diet usually consists of a greater proportion of seed than that of tree-dwelling parrots. A ground-feeding Australian cockatoo, well known for its habit of picking up grit from the roads, is the Galah or Roseate. Many birds, probably mainly young ones, are killed by vehicles as a result.

Different types and sizes of grit are available, prepared specially for cage birds. For example, one type consists mainly of crushed oyster shells, perhaps with the addition of charcoal, and another type is known as mineral grit and contains various particles that provide ingredients such as calcium, iodine, and lime. As most seed diets are deficient in minerals, grit can play an important role in supplementing the diet. The grit should be provided in small containers that are emptied and refilled regularly .

Grit should be limited for sick birds and those that have formerly been deprived of it and might take too much.

One valuable function of grit is that it can break down a foreign body of reasonable size that reaches the gizzard. This was demonstrated to me in a seven-and-a-half-week-old macaw chick that I was hand-rearing. When it and its sibling were small, I was in the habit of using a plastic spoon to feed them, which is perfectly acceptable for young chicks. I retained the habit too long and one day a predictable accident occurred. The spoon broke in the chick's mouth and it swallowed a jagged piece that was probably about 1 cm square (.15 sq in).

Not only was this chick especially dear to me, it also happened to be a Blue-throated or Caninde Macaw (*Ara glaucogularis*). I was aghast at my stupidity. However, the piece of plastic never appeared in the

feces and I felt there was a good chance it would stay in the gizzard. I therefore fed the young macaw a little grit once a week, and he suffered no ill effects.

GROUND PARROT (*Pezoporus wallicus*)
The single member of this genus, also known as the Swamp Parrot, is most closely related to the Night Parrot. The Ground Parrot's plumage is green, mottled with black and yellow, but the much longer tail and narrow red frontal band distinguish it from the Night Parrot. In length it is about 30 cm (12 in).

It is found in coastal regions of southwestern and southeastern Australia, and also in Tasmania. It

lives in heath sedge and buttongrass, hence where there is thick cover and suitable food plants. It feeds on the seeds of grasses (such as buttongrass), moving around quickly, and pulling down plant stems to bring the seeding heads near to the ground. Sometimes these birds scratch in the soil with both feet, then probe with their bills for other items of food, perhaps germinating seeds. Ground Parrots have long legs and run quickly, without the waddling gait of most parrots.

This species lays three or four eggs. The nest is a cup-shaped structure, perhaps at the base of a tussock of buttongrass. Chicks have dense, dark gray down and pink bills.

This species has been kept in captivity only rarely in Australia, but not elsewhere. The diet

The Ground Parrot lives in grassy heaths and its mottled green plumage is good camouflage. Its long legs are well adapted to a terrestrial life.

consists of sunflower and canary seed, millet, and greens, such as alfalfa and milk thistle. One keeper of the Ground Parrot described it as an uninteresting aviary bird because it was mainly nocturnal, even bathing in the middle of the night.

GUAIABERO

The Guaiabero (*Bolbospittacus lunulatus*), a small, stocky parrot of 15 cm (6 in), is the only member of its genus. The tail is very short and rounded. Its throat and cheeks are blue. In the male, the area surrounding the eyes and the nuchal collar are also blue. Both sexes are otherwise green, with a yellow patch on the underside of the secondary wing feathers. The beak is bluish-gray and the iris of the eye is dark brown. The Guaiabero originates in the Philippines.

Although common in the wild, this species is virtually unknown in aviculture, because it is very difficult to establish in captivity. In 1987, importers in Europe received this species for the first time. A Danish importer, who received ten birds in good condition, had no problems in persuading them to eat. They did not take seed, but consumed figs, apple, orange, carrots, berries, and rose hips with relish. Regrettably, they survived only a very short time, between one and three weeks. It appeared that they had died not of disease, but of malnutrition.

In the wild they are known to feed on berries and fruits, especially guavas (from which their name is derived), so the fruits offered to captive birds must be deficient in some vital nutrient. The San Diego Zoo kept two alive, one for six months and another for eight months, in 1962. The Swiss aviculturist Dr R. Burkard also kept this species for a short while. His specimens fed on potato, sweet potato, and fruit. They were described as quiet and slow moving, but liable to fly off suddenly and injure themselves if startled.

Those received in Denmark were described as very beautiful, of the same shade of green as male Eclectus Parrots and the same size as *Psittaculirostris* Fig Parrots. Their behavior is said to be not unlike that of Fig Parrots.

H

HABITAT

Parrots are essentially birds of the tropics, where they occur in many different types of habitat. However, not all parrots originate from hot or warm climates. There are a considerable number of mountain species that spend most of their lives at high altitudes, even in forest covered by low cloud. Chicks of many parrot species have thick down, to keep them warm when nights are cold, or days are cool.

The species with the most southerly distribution is the Austral Conure (*Enicognathus f. ferrugineus*) from the coldest part of South America – Tierra del Fuego, where the climate is bleak and hostile. In New Zeland, the Kea (*Nestor notabilis*) is found in the New Zealand Alps, where it plays in the snow!

Even species that inhabit Caribbean islands can spend most of their days in a cool temperature; for example, the St. Vincent Parrot (*Amazona guildingii*) lives only in the mountains, where it has been pushed to higher altitudes by human encroachment; once this parrot occurred throughout the island. Here, cloud cover results in quite chilly temperatures for most of the day.

Tropical rain forest, however, is the type of habitat in which species and individual parrots are most plentiful. The climate is hot, varies little throughout the year, and produces an abundance of food at all times. Some species are found in a wide variety of habitats throughout their range, whereas others have very specialized requirements. For example, the numerous and widely distributed Orange-winged Amazon is found in rain forest, mangrove forest, savannah forest, timbered coastal sand ridges, and cacao plantations.

In contrast, the Tucuman Amazon (*A. tucumana*), from Bolivia and Argentina, is a bird of forests of alder (*Alnus jorullensis*). The closely related Pretre's Amazon (*A. pretrei*), from southeastern Brazil and northeastern Argentina, is found only in forests of *Araucaria* (a kind of pine), and the seeds of this tree are its most favored food.

Some species are nomadic, moving about according to the food supply. One of the most nomadic species of northern Australia, for example, is the cockatiel (*Nymphicus hollandicus*). These birds' roaming is most marked during dry seasons, when they may suddenly appear in areas where they have not been seen for years.

Some species have highly specialized habitats. Among the Grass Parakeets (*Neophemas*), the Rock Parakeet (*N. petrophila*) is found only among coastal sand dunes and offshore rocky islets of southern Australia. The least specialized member of the genus is the Blue-winged Parakeet (*N. chrysostoma*) from southeastern Australia and Tasmania. It, too, occurs in coastal sand dunes, and also in saltbush plains, forest, sparsely timbered grasslands, and acacia scrublands.

In many parts of Australia parrots and humans live in close, but not happy, association. Parrots are considered to be pests that destroy crops, especially grain. Cockatoos destroy more than crops; they even descend on houses and vandalize the wooden roofs. They are extremely unpopular, and shooting and poisoning are accepted methods of exterminating them. Despite this, parrots can be seen in many city parks and gardens.

In many parts of the tropics, however, parrots live quite happily in close association with humans.

In many South American towns, parrots are as numerous as people in the main squares. In Leticia, Colombia, I saw a huge flock of Canary-winged Parakeets leave their roost in such a location at first light, and in São Paulo, in a small park surrounded by skyscrapers, another *Brotogeris* parakeet, the All-green (*B. tirica*) can be observed.

I well remember looking out of the window of a hotel in the Andes of Colombia, to see a tiny Spectacled Parrotlet (*Forpus conspicillatus*) perched on a stark lamppost. It seemed so incongruous.

In India, the Ringneck Parakeet (*Psittacula krameri*) is very common in the vicinity of the larger cities, such as New Delhi, and is seen in gardens and orchards.

In short, parrots will be found in almost any location that provides food and nest sites.

HANDLING

All species of parrots, even the small ones, can bite very hard, and most will not hesitate to do so when handled. When catching a parrot, the aim is to immobilize the mandibles by placing a thumb and forefinger on either side of the beak. It is often difficult to maintain this grip, as the large species are very strong; thus it is best to transfer the bird to a towel at once, keeping the mandibles closed.

It is much easier to control a bird held within a towel and to catch one by putting a towel over its head, yet retaining one's grip on its beak. A proper catching net should

Only young parrots such as the Leadbeater's Cockatoos shown here can be handled in such a casual manner.

70

be used to remove birds from an aviary. Gloves are not recommended for catching and handling; they frighten parrots and make it difficult for the handler to hold the bird efficiently.

HAND-REARING

Rearing parrot chicks by hand is very time-consúming and limits one's other activities; abandoned chicks are often better placed with foster parents. However, chicks are often hand-reared because the tame young that result are in great demand as pets. A brooder is essential in a cool climate. In a warm climate a heating pad may suffice.

A spoon with the sides bent inwards is the best implement for feeding. The food must be warm and fairly runny; if unsure of the correct consistency, it is better to add more water than give food that is too thick. The frequency of feedings will vary according to the size and crop capacity of the chick (those that have been fed by their parents, or by other birds, usually have a larger capacity). The crop should never be filled to the maximum, even though this means feeding more often.

Newly hatched chicks will need to be fed every hour and a half on very liquid food, and those approaching weaning should be fed every three or four hours on thicker food. Feedings should be given between about 6:30 a.m. and 11 p.m., if possible.

Hand-rearing is a very complex subject that cannot be covered in a few paragraphs. Many different foods are used, according to the species and the inclination of the feeder. These and other aspects are covered fully in *Hand-rearing Parrots* by Rosemary Low, published by Blandford Press in 1987. (For information on this book, contact Sterling Publishing Co., Inc., 2 Park Avenue, New York, N.Y. 10016.)

Foods commonly used consist of a mixture of dry baby cereal (at least 15% protein) and some fruit, either fresh, such as papaya or apple, or canned baby foods, adding wheat germ cereal and sunflower seed kernels (available from health food stores) at about ten days. These items should be mixed with water in a blender, then cooked or heated well.

A spoon with the sides bent inwards is the best instrument for hand-feeding a chick, such as this Iris Lorikeet (*Trichoglossus iris*).

Supplements such as calcium should be added to the spoon as the food is given, since heating can destroy their value. Vitamins are given in exceptional cases; the vitamin content of a regular diet should be adequate.

Weaning from soft food to seed should be a very gradual process and can take as long as eight months to accomplish in large species such as macaws, although most parrots will be weaned by four to five months, or sooner in the small species. Foods enjoyed by chicks being weaned include corn on the cob, soaked sunflower seed, bread, millet spray, apples, and papaya.

HANGING PARROTS (*Loriculus*)

Hanging Parrots could be described as the tiny gems of the parrot family. Their feeding and care demand a little more time than that of most parrots, but the pleasure provided by their beauty, diminutiveness, and interesting behavior is worth the extra effort.

The name is derived from the fact that these birds normally roost hanging upside down, from the wire roof of an aviary or from a perch. However, a breeder of several species of *Loriculus* told me that some female Philippine Hanging Parrots in his collection do not roost in this way, and that neither do birds that are sick.

These tiny birds, measuring 11–12 cm (4⅓–4¾ in), are mainly green, with a red beak, and orange or black and contrasting colors on the throat and/or crown and on the upper tail coverts. Aviculturally, they should be regarded more like softbills than parrots, and are seen at their best in a planted aviary, with softbills or finches.

Hanging Parrots can be kept and

bred on the colony system, but because they need live food when rearing young, and the competition for this food is too great in a mixed aviary, the best breeding results will be achieved when each pair have an enclosure to themselves.

There is a subtle or marked degree of sexual dimorphism, according to the species, which originate in Asia, Indonesia, and New Guinea.

The most commonly imported species is the Vernal Hanging Parrot (*L. vernalis*), which has a wide area of distribution, including India, Burma, Assam, Thailand, the Malay Peninsula, Cambodia, Laos, and Vietnam. A common species, it feeds on fruits, berries, small seeds, and nectar. It is light green, with a pale blue patch on the throat and a red rump and tail coverts. The only sexual distinction is the eye color, the iris being white in the male and brown in the female.

In my opinion, the most beautiful species – indeed, one of the most exquisite of all small parrots – is the Blue-crowned Hanging Parrot (*L. galgulus*). Its brilliant colors are unrivaled, as is the texture of its feathers, and the almost luminous quality of the red in the plumage. The tiny black beak adds to its beauty: the overall effect is one of neatness found in few other psittacines.

Both sexes have a blue patch on the crown and a triangular patch of tawny gold on the mantle, which are duller in the female. Rump and upper tail coverts, perhaps the most beautiful feature of the species, are scarlet; also the throat in the male is also scarlet.

A Danish breeder told me that this species can be sexed at about six months, when the blue on the male's head starts to appear. At this stage an immature male can be distinguished from an adult female by his brighter scarlet rump. The red on the throat is the last color to appear. By the age of one year, the male is in full adult plumage.

Also available is the Philippine Hanging Parrot (*L. philippensis*). This is the largest Hanging Parrot, of which there are 11 subspecies. In *L. philippensis philippensis*, the forehead and crown are red, followed by a dusky yellow patch; the nape is decorated with a golden-orange band. The male has a large red patch on the throat, and the female has pale blue lores. Immature birds have very little red on the forehead.

The other six species are very rare in captivity. One which was virtually unknown until 1984 is the Celebes or Red-crowned Hanging Parrot (*L. stigmatus*) from the islands of the Celebes in Indonesia. A vivid shade of green, the male's plumage is set off by a scarlet forehead, crown, throat, rump, and tail coverts. The beak is black and the iris pale yellow. The female is all green, with the iris brown. Immature birds are mainly green, slightly darker above, with a tiny orange spot on the throat. The rump is red and the tail, as in the adults, is light blue on the underside.

Because their diet consists partly of fruit, which is flicked in all directions, it would be advisable to keep these birds indoors only in a cage made specially for them. It should be constructed of a material, such as plastic, that is easy to clean, and perhaps have the front made of glass. Ease of cleaning should also be borne in mind in a small aviary. In a large enclosure their feeding habits are not a problem.

A wide variety of foods should be offered, with unlimited fruit for newly imported birds, as well as boiled sweetened rice, which many are offered in the country of export. When half an apple is provided, only the thin shell of the skin will be left. All the usual fruits, nectar, or sponge cake and nectar, small seeds, such as canary and soaked or sprouted sunflower seed (small), spray millet, and pure fruit juices will be taken. One breeder provides his Hanging Parrots with yogurt blended with sugar, pollen meal with glucose, and peas, plus various fruits.

Protein, preferably of animal origin, is essential when young are being reared. Ants' eggs and mealworms, dusted with a multivitamin and mineral preparation, are the best forms of live food: maggots introduce a risk of botulism unless cleaned for several days in bran or sand.

The nest box provided for these birds should have a small base, about 11 cm (4½ in) square, but should be high enough to allow the birds to line it with a deep layer of leaves. These are necessary to keep the nest dry during the rearing period. Females will carry leaves into the nest in the feathers of the breast or rump. At Loro Parque, where only pine branches are provided, a female Philippine Hanging Parrot lined her nest with small pieces of pine.

Courtship behavior is fascinating to observe. I am impelled to stop and watch if I pass the Blue-crowns' aviary when the male is displaying. It is a wonderful sight: the red feathers of the throat seem to be inflated. Most extraordinary of all is the manner in which the male feeds the female. A globule of food protrudes from his beak, almost like a child blowing bubble gum, and is sucked in by the female. Hanging Parrots lay three, and occasionally four, eggs, which are incubated by the female for 20 days. The young spend just under five weeks in the nest.

These small birds should not be expected to tolerate low temperatures. A heated shelter or indoor accommodation should be provided in the winter.

HATCHING FAILURE
There are many reasons why eggs fail to hatch, and it is usually very difficult to determine which factor is responsible. Death of the embryo during any stage of incubation could be due to dirty conditions in the nest, resulting in bacteria entering the egg. A dietary deficiency of a vital element can kill the embryo. This is why a mineral and vitamin supplement is recommended for females prior to laying. It should be added to a popular item of food with which it will easily combine, such as bread and milk, not given in the drinking water where it will affect the taste more noticeably, possibly resulting in the bird's not drinking.

Death of the embryo due to insufficient humidity is rarer than was formerly believed. In fact, many parrot eggs that are artificially incubated require little or no water during incubation, until the chick pips the shell, when humidity should be greatly increased.

Excessive humidity is a common cause of embryonic death. An egg must lose about 16% of its weight through evaporation during incubation; if the environment is too wet, this is impossible and the embryo dies. Weight loss is also related to the pore structure of the eggshell; eggs with very porous shells seldom hatch unless they are weighed daily and the humidity within the incubator is controlled to maintain the correct weight loss.

Thin-shelled eggs usually fail to hatch, either because they are unintentionally damaged by the incubating bird (who may then be blamed for egg-breaking) or because there is insufficient calcium available for the developing embryo which draws on the calcium within the eggshell.

Dead-in-shell is the term for chicks that die in the egg, fully formed, and just prior to hatching. It is not correct to use this term for the death of the embryo at an earlier stage. Low environmental temperature is one of the most common causes of dead-in-shell and is all too prevalent in birds breeding in outdoor aviaries during the winter.

A not uncommon cause of

A Solomon Eclectus Parrot (*Eclectus roratus solomonensis*) in the final stages of hatching.

Assisted hatching.

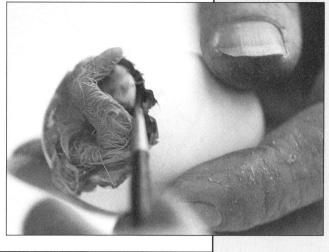

hatching failure is that the egg membrane (the layer between the chick and the shell) is so firmly attached to the chick's head that the chick is unable to rotate within the egg in order to hatch. I have removed many parrot chicks from the egg in these circumstances: they would have died unless assisted. All have grown into excellent specimens, so the reason for potential hatching failure in this case is not that the chick is weak. If assistance in hatching is too late, the chick will die because it has used up all the available oxygen and its brain suffers damage.

Incidentally, the period from pipping to hatching varies tremendously, from a few hours to as long as three days.

Eggs that fail to hatch because they are infertile cannot be distinguished from those in which the embryo dies during the first few hours of incubation. About 25% of all embryonic deaths are believed to occur during the first three to five days of incubation.

The reasons for infertility are that mating has not occurred, or it has occurred, but one, or both, birds are not in full breeding condition. A problem with many parrots, especially Amazons, is that male and female do not simultaneously achieve breeding condition. Another cause of infertile eggs, in adult birds as well as inexperienced young ones, is that the male has not learned to copulate correctly.

HAWK-HEADED PARROT
(*Deroptyus accipitrinus accipitrinus*)
The single member of this genus is one of the most distinctive of parrots. It is recognized by its erectile head feathers of maroon margined with blue, a color scheme that is repeated on the underparts. The head feathers are brown, prominently shaft-streaked with buff. The feathers of the forehead are whitish in *D. accipitrinus accipitrinus* and dusky brown in the subspecies *fuscifrons*. The upperparts are green. Immature birds have some green on the head and the blue margins of the feathers are more greenish.

In length it is about 31 cm (12 in). Plumage is alike in male and female.

This intelligent species comes from the Amazon basin (the

Guianas, northern Brazil, Colombia, and northeastern Peru), where it occurs in small groups. Occasionally imported, it has never been common in aviculture and breeding successes are not frequent. Compatibility can be a problem, as adult birds can be extremely aggressive (towards humans as well as other Hawk-heads). When two are introduced, there should be two feeding points in the aviary to ensure that one bird is not kept away from the food by the other, dominant one.

The threat display of the Hawk-headed Parrot is spectacular: the maroon and blue head feathers are erected to form a ruff and the bird sways from side to side in a menacing manner, emitting a whining sound. This would undoubtedly be effective in frightening off enemies.

Hawk-heads require a diet containing much fresh fruit, in addition to seeds such as sunflower, canary, millet, buckwheat, spray millet, and the usual vegetables and berries; hawthorn berries are especially relished. Bread and milk can also be offered, especially when the birds are breeding.

This is a nervous parrot that is not easy to breed. If successful, two or three eggs are laid and incubated by the female for about

The Hawk-headed Parrot (*Deroptyus accipitrinus accipitrinus*) is most distinctive in plumage and behavior.

74

26 days. The young leave the nest after about nine weeks. Hand-reared young are delightful, as tame Hawk-heads can be endearingly affectionate.

It should be noted that this species can be extremely noisy.

A nest box should always be available for roosting.

HYACINTHINE MACAW
(*Anodorhynchus hyacinthinus*)

Named for its color of hyacinth blue, this is the largest of all parrots, and also one of the most magnificent. Its appearance evokes more gasps of admiration and surprise in those seeing it for the first time than almost any other parrot. Its sheer size, and that of its beak, are awe-inspiring.

In length it is about 100 cm (39 in), and it weighs about 1,250–1,400 g (42½–47½ oz). The eyes and lower mandible are surrounded by bright yellow skin. Lear's Macaw (*A. leari*) has a similar coloration, but is smaller, only about 75 cm (30 in). The mysterious Glaucous Macaw (*A. glaucus*) is said to be extinct, not having been recorded in the wild since the 19th century. It resembled the Lear's Macaw, except for the slightly different shade of its plumage.

The Hyacinthine Macaw originates from the interior of Brazil, south of the Amazon, and also from extreme eastern Bolivia and northeastern Paraguay. It is declining because of the volume of trade and disturbance of its habitat, much of which has been settled in recent years. The origin of Lear's Macaw was discovered as recently as 1978, in northeastern Bahia in Brazil. Only one population is known to exist; it consists of about 100 birds, and possibly fewer.

A tame Hyacinthine Macaw is remarkably docile. It could sever a finger as easily as a person could break a match, yet is gentle and affectionate, with a doglike devotion to its human friends. Hand-reared birds are in demand as pets – among those able to afford one. Few parrots command a higher price. Equally, few people can afford the time or the accommodation needed for such a demanding and beautiful creature.

It is to be hoped that many Hyacinthine Macaws obtained as pets are given the opportunity to breed when mature, or, certainly in the United States, the future of the species in aviculture will not be secure.

An increase of animal protein (cooked meat, hard-boiled egg, canned dog food) may encourage these birds to breed. The normal diet should include plenty of large nuts (especially walnuts and Brazil nuts) and sunflower seed. Newly imported birds may have to be offered coconut if they refuse all other foods. The diet should also contain corn on the cob, dog biscuits, or those made for other animals, such as ZuPreem (Zu/Preem, Hill's Division Riviana Foods Inc, POB 148, Topeka, KS 66601), plenty of fruit, sweetcorn, peas, boiled beans, and sprouted wheat and/or oats. One pair consumed large amounts of green hazel nuts after their chick was six weeks old.

Captive-bred females will lay as early as four or five years old. Nest sites used in captivity have included a steel drum (227 liters/50-gal), a whiskey barrel mounted on its side, and strong wooden nest boxes. The two eggs are incubated by the female for 28 or 29 days. The young resemble the adults, except for a paler yellow skin and slightly duller plumage. When rearing young, Hyacinthines need plenty of limestone or large grit.

This species is being bred in an increasing number of American and European collections. The

The Hyacinthine Macaw (*Anodorhynchus hyacinthinus*) has the most massive bill of any parrot; the bill's strength is enormous.

young are very aware, intelligent, and lovable. Their enormous feet at the fledgling stage lend them an air of ungainly charm!

Lear's Macaw is extremely rare in captivity; only about 12 birds are known outside Brazil. These include only one breeding pair, at Busch Gardens, Tampa, Florida. The male of this pair had been on exhibit at Parrot Jungle in Miami for 27 years before being sent to Tampa in 1982. Within two months of their introduction, the female laid three eggs that were infertile. Two young from this pair survive (off-exhibit) at Busch gardens.

HYGIENE
Hygiene is a vitally important part of good management. Many bird keepers do not realize how important hygiene is until a bird dies as a result of a bacterial disease, or worse, an outbreak occurs that kills a number of birds. Disease can be introduced to the occupants of an outdoor aviary by wild birds whose feces fall into the enclosure – so no matter how clean one keeps it, there is always this risk.

However, when the occupants' feces are allowed to accumulate, and mould grows on them and on discarded food, there is a danger of a fungus disease. Cages contaminated by the droppings of mice or wild birds could be a source of pseudotuberculosis, for example, so regular cleaning and disinfection are necessary. A veterinarian or pet store can recommend a suitable disinfectant for outdoor aviaries and bird rooms.

Cleanliness must also extend to receptacles for food and water, perches, and nest boxes.

Food and water containers must be cleaned daily.

ILLNESS
The symptoms of ill health to watch for are inactivity, sleepiness, frequent blinking of the eyes, dull eyes, ruffled feathers and an impression that the bird feels cold, discharge from the eyes and/or nostrils, soiled vent feathers, and general weakness. Most sick birds rest with two feet on the perch (instead of one foot as is normal in adult birds), while the head is tucked into the feathers of the back.

Other symptoms are **1** lack of appetite; if much food remains in the dish when normally it is empty, this is an immediate cause for concern, and **2** feces that differ from normal in color and consistency. Remember, however, that certain items of food can also produce this effect.

The priorities for a sick bird are warmth (see *INFRARED LAMP*), isolation, to prevent the spread of disease and also to ensure that the bird is undisturbed, veterinary attention, and suitable food. A sick bird may have to be tempted to eat by offering favorite items, or it may require a soft food, such as bread and milk, even although it does not normally take this. If it refuses food it may have to be force-fed (see *FORCE-FEEDING*).

See also *STRESS, WINTER CARE* and *ANTIBIOTICS*.

INCUBATION
The embryo within an egg can develop only if it is maintained at the correct temperature; in parrots this is approximately 37°C (99°F). Incubation is the process of applying heat to the egg. Heat is applied via the brood patch, an area on the abdomen of the bird. When it lowers itself onto the eggs, it ruffles the feathers in that area to expose the patch. In most parrots, only the female incubates; in others, notably cockatoos (and also some *Vini* and *Charmosyna* lories), both sexes share incubation duties.

The incubation period in parrots varies from 14 to 29 days under optimum conditions, depending upon the species. In cold weather a species with a normal incubation period of 23 days, could have that period prolonged by three or even four days. Likewise, in hot weather, the incubation period could be shortened by one or two days. Such information can be obtained only by the study of birds in captivity.

By far the shortest incubation period of any parrot is that of the Lesser Vasa (*Coracopsis nigra*) – only 14 days. It is possible that the same applies to the Greater Vasa (*C. vasa*), but this species has yet to be bred in captivity and nothing is known about it in the wild. (In many respects, the *Coracopsis* species are aberrant; they are not truly representative members of the parrot family, in my opinion.)

The next shortest incubation periods are those recorded in Australian parakeets: that for the budgerigar is 18 days, for others it is usually 19 days.

The longest incubation period, of about 29 days, is found in some cockatoos and in the Hyacinthine Macaw. Here, perhaps, I may be permitted to correct Joseph Forshaw who, in his excellent book *Parrots of the World*, states: "Duration of incubation varies roughly in proportion to the size of the bird; for small parrots it is from seventeen to twenty-three days, but for the large macaws it can be up to five weeks."

Many lories have an incubation period of 25 days, from the smallest *Vini* to the largest *Lorius*, size range 17–31 cm (6½–12 in), although in most *Trichoglossus*, which are medium in size, the incubation period is 23 days. There are many other examples to disprove the size theory.

It must be remembered that not all parrots commence to incubate when the first egg is laid, although the female may be in the nest from this time. Also, unless the eggs in the clutch are marked as laid, and all the eggs hatch, it may be difficult to obtain accurate records of incubation periods. In fact, the only way is to place a newly laid egg in an incubator.

The incubation period is actually defined as the length of time from the laying of the last egg in the clutch to the hatching of that egg, assuming that there are no interruptions, other than the normal few minutes' absence from the nest by the incubating bird.

During the incubation period, most eggs lose about 16% of their weight, because of water loss from the contents through the porous shell. The eggshell porosity of species that nest at high altitudes is reduced, to compensate for the changes in embryonic respiratory gas exchange and water loss from the egg as a consequence of low barometric pressure. Breeders who use an incubator must therefore bear in mind that humidity requirements within the incubator may vary according to the species.

INCUBATORS

The number of models available to aviculturists has increased greatly in recent years. It may therefore be difficult to make a choice. The following guidelines are suggested:

1 Choose a model that is made by a well-established company and that has been in use for some years. One sees various makes come and go, especially at the low end of the price range. Some appear to have been produced without sufficient testing.

2 Choose a small model. Large incubators, with a capacity of 1,000 eggs or more, are ideal for commercial poultry breeders, but they operate best when full. Few private breeders will require an incubator with a capacity of more than 30 or 40 eggs. In any case, it is more practical to use several small incubators, because each one can be kept at a different humidity, thereby giving better control for the requirements of individual eggs.

3 Choose an incubator that is easy to keep clean.

4 Choose a model with the heat source in the center. Failing this, place the thermometer as near the eggs as possible, or an accurate temperature reading will not be obtained.

5 Choose a forced-air model. Few still-air incubators are available these days, because the temperature fluctuations are unacceptable in such models. If a still-air incubator is used, the temperature (see *INCUBATION*) will need to be 2 or 3° F higher than that recommended for forced-air machines.

My own recommendation for the

small breeder would be a Marsh Farms Turn-X or the larger Roll-X. Most incubators have automatic turning devices. These are useful for people who are unable to turn eggs at frequent intervals (at least four times a day is recommended). However you may prefer to turn the eggs by hand (as I do) as some models might not treat the eggs as gently as one would wish.

Do not keep an incubator in a room that is subject to temperature fluctuations, such as a kitchen. Avoid situations where the sun could strike the incubator, thus increasing the temperature. Keep the incubator out of reach of children and animals. Ensure that an accurate thermometer is used. Those fitted to many incubators are either inaccurate or difficult to read, or both. A digital thermometer is recommended (see *BROODERS*).

Ensure that the incubator is sterilized or fumigated between

This virtually unbreakable ceramic infrared lamp that emits heat without light, is ideal for use with sick birds.

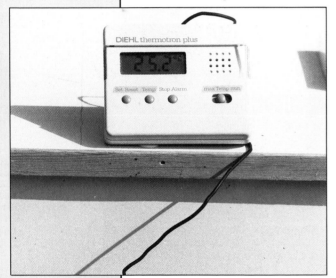

A digital thermometer is recommended for brooder and incubator: it is very quick to register any change in temperature and also easy to read.

hatches. Fumigation can be carried out as follows: place a pinch of crystals of potassium permanganate in a small container inside the incubator. Then add a teaspoonful of formaldehyde (37% solution) to the crystals. Close the lid and leave the room quickly, because a very powerful and unpleasant gas is given off. Leave alone for 24 hours.

INFRARED LAMP
Unless the temperature is already in the region of 30°C (86°F), the first step to take when a bird is unwell is to place it in warm surroundings. This should not be

by a radiator as is sometimes recommended, but near a concentrated source of heat from which the bird can move away if it desires. The best source is undoubtedly an infrared lamp. Hospital cages for parrots are seldom practical; in any case their even temperature does not allow the occupant to escape excessive heat, and also the atmosphere is extremely dry.

There are various types of infrared lamps, such as the shortwave emitters made of glass. These are useful, but not the best. The bright glare of the lamp is not restful for a sick bird, the glass is vulnerable to explosion and breakage (especially as a result of being splashed by water), and some of the energy is dissipated as light. Possibly, also, the vitamin content of the food in the cage is destroyed.

The type of infrared lamp that I have used for years, and that I would never be without, is the dull emitter (no light) with a ceramic element. It is virtually unbreakable, unaffected by water splashes, and has an extremely long life (the bright emitter does not). The low filament temperature eliminates fire risk.

K

KAKA (*Nestor meridionalis*)

This bird originates in New Zealand. It shows sexual dimorphism in that the bill is usually longer and more curved in the male. In length it is about 45 cm (18 in). It is extremely rare in captivity.

The Kaka is a large and unusually colored bird, mainly greenish-brown with the rump and upper and undertail coverts crimson barred with dark brown. The ear coverts are orange-yellow, and the underwing coverts and the underside of the flight feathers are scarlet. In immature birds the base of the lower mandible is yellow.

Kakas were kept at the London Zoo as long ago as 1863, but none had been seen outside New Zealand in this century until the Stuttgart Zoo, in West Germany, received a pair in 1986. These were bred in New Zealand, in the Auckland Zoo, which has been consistently successful in rearing Kakas since 1981.

The three or four eggs are incubated for 28 days. Newly hatched chicks are covered in white down, and spend nine or ten weeks in the nest.

In captivity Kakas feed on seeds, fruits, and vegetables, and also on nectar and brown bread. Nectar is an important part of their diet in the wild. When feeding on pollen in the wild, some pollen adheres to their heads, resulting in cross-pollination of flax and other plants. Kakas also consume harmful insects and grubs and therefore play an important role in the ecology of the New Zealand forests. With their long hooked beaks they dig out large grubs, such as those of the corn beetle, which are 10–13 cm (4–5 in) in length.

Unfortunately, because of deforestation, Kakas have declined appreciably in the wild.

KAKAPO (*Strigops habroptilus*)

The Kakapo is one of the most interesting birds in existence, and sadly it is also one of the most endangered. A number of features of appearance and behavior make it unique among parrots – even unique among birds. The heaviest parrot, 1–3.4 kg (2–7½ lb) – males being heavier than females – it is large, over 60 cm (2 ft) in length, with a short tail. The soft plumage is barred and streaked throughout with brown and yellow, being mainly green above and greenish-yellow below. Its normal stance is near-horizontal.

Flightless and mainly nocturnal, it is also a *lek* species, the only lek parrot and the only flightless lek bird. Lek is a mating system in which males congregate and perform displays on traditionally established grounds. The male has an inflatable thoracic air sac with which it produces a booming call, the aim of which is to attract a female. (As many as 1,000 booms per hour have been recorded.) Booming does not occur every year, but only when breeding attempts are made – probably only when food is sufficient.

Alas, the number of females left in existence is so small that, despite the heroic efforts of the New Zealand Wildlife Service, the species is on the very brink of extinction. It evolved in the absence of mammalian predators, and, being flightless and nesting on the ground, it has not been equipped to cope with the subsequent occurrence of these predators.

Historically, the Kakapo's biggest enemy was humans. At one time Kakapo was the principal food of the Maoris. They also hunted it relentlessly for its highly prized skins; cloaks were made from the feathers. When the European settlers arrived, this magnificent parrot was exterminated in most areas – by intentional killing and through the introduction of rats, stoats, cats, and dogs.

Today, the population numbers in the region of forty individuals. Since the late 1970s intensive efforts have been made to protect the survivors of one of the most fascinating species ever to have evolved.

KAKARIKIS (*Cyanoramphus*)

Kakarikis, perhaps the most active parrots existing, make delightful aviary birds. Found only in New Zealand and its offshore islands, there are two species, the Red-fronted (*C. novaezelandiae*), which measures about 28 cm (11 in), and the Yellow-fronted (*C. auriceps*) which is about 25 cm (9¾ in) long. The latter also has a red forehead, but is immediately identified by the yellow area behind the red. Immature birds have a brown iris (red in adults) and, in the Red-fronted, less red on the head.

Kakarikis are fearless and inquisitive in the extreme (escape soon follows if a hole develops in the aviary). Members of this genus are usually exceptionally prolific. They mature earlier than any other parrot of comparable size and have been known to produce young at only five months old. They need a fairly large nest, approximately 23–25 cm (9–9¾ in) square and 31 cm (12 in) high, to accommodate what could be a very large family.

As many as 10 or 11 chicks have been hatched in one clutch. However, the usual clutch is five to nine eggs, and the incubation period is about 19 days. The young spend five to six weeks in the nest. During this period a rearing food must be provided in addition to the usual seeds, fruits, and vegetables. Mealworms will be enjoyed during this time. A very wide range of foods will be eaten, especially greens of all kinds, a fresh turf of grass, and the berries of hawthorn and elder.

Kakarikis spend a lot of time on the ground, scratching and picking up items of food: they are therefore very susceptible to worms and must be wormed at least twice a year. Long-legged birds, they can run very fast (also up and down welded mesh), without the waddling gait of most parrots that have short legs.

Kakarikis can be unreservedly recommended to beginners (who will enjoy their prolificacy) and to more experienced breeders. Their pleasant voices will not disturb anyone and their friendly personalities always give pleasure. They are not destructive or aggressive and can even be kept with small birds such as finches, but they should not be kept with other parrots, who will be annoyed by their inquisitive antics.

KEA (*Nestor notabilis*)
In its large size – 48cm (19 in) –

bronze-green plumage, and elongated beak, the Kea is quite unlike any other parrot in aviculture. The most colorful areas of the plumage, the orange-red rump and underwing coverts, are seldom visible when the bird is perched. The bill is usually shorter and less curved in the female.

An inhabitant of the mountains of New Zealand's South Island, Keas are noted for their inquisitive and playful habits. A century ago, they had a reputation as sheep killers, and a bounty was placed on their heads. Thousands were killed. However, far from becoming extinct, as some predicted, they remain fairly common to this day and are now partly protected. It would be a tragedy if this endearing and highly intelligent parrot were to become extinct.

They are fascinating aviary birds, often bounding sideways along the ground with their heads cocked upwards. Vocally, they are unlike any other parrot, and their distinctive quavering cry can be heard throughout the night as well as during the day. In the wild they nest on the ground, in crevices among rocks or tree roots; in an aviary a nest site can be made out of rocks or a horizontal nest box placed on the ground. They will use a box at a higher level also.

Three or four eggs are laid and incubated for about 29 days. The young spend about ten weeks in the nest. Animal protein, in the form of meat, young mice, and mealworms, is required during the rearing period. They will eat almost anything in the way of table scraps (meat, potatoes, rice, bread) and also root vegetables, such as whole carrots and beetroot. The wider the variety of items offered, the better.

The Kea is not common in captivity outside New Zealand, being bred in comparatively few collections, and therefore it is expensive to purchase. They are endearing and amusing, and anyone fortunate enough to own a pair should make every effort to persuade them to breed.

KING PARAKEETS (*Alisterus*)
The Kings are extremely beautiful parakeets with long, broad tails. One species comes from Australia, one from New Guinea, and a third, with a distinctive subspecies, from

Indonesia. Only the Australian King Parakeet is fairly common in captivity.

To be seen at their best they need a spacious aviary, 5–6 m (16–19½ ft) long. However, when the young fledge in an enclosure of this length, precautions must be taken to prevent their flying at speed into the wire and killing themselves. A protective mass of branches should be placed in front of the welded mesh.

King Parakeets accept a varied diet of the usual seeds, pine nuts, greens, and fruit. A rearing food, spray millet, fresh corn on the cob, and extra greens should be offered when young are being reared. Rose hips and berries of hawthorn and elder are also eaten.

Kings lay two to four eggs, or up to five in the Australian species. The incubation period is 21 days and the young remain in the nest for about eight weeks. They are not among the easiest birds to breed, yet some pairs can prove prolific. A pair of Green-winged Kings, of the subspecies *moszkowskii*, hatched nine young in three nests in 1987 at Loro Parque. The second nest of three were reared by the parents, but the other chicks were removed for hand-rearing.

There was a sad sequel to this wonderful performance. When the rain came in October, it stimulated the male to nest again, but the female was not in breeding condition. He attacked her and she died from the head injuries she received. This is a problem of which owners of King Parakeets should be constantly aware – although it is not necessarily the male who is the aggressor in the island Kings. It is often necessary to cut the flight feathers of the male when a new female is introduced, to prevent her being chased and stressed.

The Australian King (*A. scapularis*) is the largest, with a length of about 40 cm (15½ in). The male is green with scarlet head and underparts; the female's head is green and she is duller throughout, as are immature birds. A yellow mutation has been bred.

The Green-winged King (*A. chloropterus*) from New Guinea is a very striking bird. It is rare in aviculture and very expensive. Slightly smaller and more slender

An Australian King Parakeet (*Alisterus scapularis*), aged 19 days.

than the Australian King, with the mantle dark blue, there is a yellowish-green patch extending along the wing coverts.

The female of the Green-winged King can be distinguished from the Australian species by her deeper blue rump and reddish tinge to the underparts. The female of the race *moszkowskii* lacks blue on the mantle, but is otherwise nearly as colorful as the male. In nest feather some young males have dark blue on the mantle; others do not.

Little known until the mid 1970s, the Amboina King Parakeet (*A. amboinensis amboinensis*) has blue on its mantle, and green wings with blue at the bend. The tail is blue above. The shade of red on head and underparts is dark. The upper mandible is red on the upper part and black on the lower half, and the lower mandible is black (as in *chloropterus*). Not common, this species is being bred in a few collections. In one, the female ignored all nest boxes until one was placed on the ground; there she reared a single chick.

A male Australian
Crimson-winged
Parakeet
(*Aprosmictus
erythropterus
erythropterus*).

Parakeets (1)

The male Barraband's Parakeet *(Polytelis swainsonii)* is one of the most elegant of all the Australian parakeets.

Above: A male Many-colored Parakeet *(Psephotus varius)*.

Young Orange-flanked Parakeets *(Brotogeris pyrrhopterus)* can be recognized by their dark beaks. The two young with this pair were bred at Loro Parque, Tenerife.

L

LEAR'S MACAW – see under *HYACINTHINE MACAW*

Leptosittaca CONURE

The single member of this genus, known as Branicki's or the Golden-plumed Conure (*L. branickii*), appears to have been separated from the *Aratinga* species only because it possesses elongated yellow feathers above the ear coverts. Mainly green, it has a narrow yellow frontal band, yellow lores, and a yellow line of feathers below the eye. The cere is partly feathered. The abdomen is mottled with orange. In length this bird is 35 cm (14 in).

Very little is known about this conure, which occurs in the Andes of Colombia, southwestern Ecuador, and central Peru. It has never been exported.

Loriculus – see *HANGING PARROTS*

LORIES

The lories and lorikeets (collectively known as lories) are a distinctive group of birds that originate from Indonesia, New Guinea, Australia, and the islands of the Pacific. In the wild the principal food of most species is pollen and nectar, but fruits are also eaten. Until recently, the captive diet for these birds has consisted of "nectar" made from such items as baby cereal and honey. When fed on this, the feces are of a liquid consistency.

Some breeders are now giving a dry diet, at least for part of the day. While the hardier species will exist on this, the delicate ones, such as the Fairy Lorikeet (*Charmosyna pulchella*), and the more conservative feeders, such as the *Chalcopsitta* lories, would starve to death rather than accept dry items as food.

The experienced breeder should be most careful about the introduction of dry foods; the danger is that beginners will be misled into believing that all lories can be maintained on such foods.

Pet store owners, or others anxious to sell lories, may try in this way to give the impression that feeding lories is no more time-consuming or specialized than that of other parrots. Anyone not prepared to go to the trouble of providing nectar should not consider keeping lories. (See *NECTAR*.)

Some lories are among the most brilliantly colored birds in existence – but they are not only colorful. Playful and lively in the extreme, they make fascinating aviary birds – showy, inquisitive, intelligent, and often free-breeding. Although the clutch size of most species is only two, they make up for this by being multiple-brooded; three or four nests a year are not uncommon. Breeders who crave the excitement of the breeding season all year round would do well to consider lories. However, young have to be hand-reared during cold weather, which they are otherwise unlikely to survive during the first few days of life.

Each pair must have an enclosure to themselves, with the exception of the little Goldie's Lorikeet (*Trichoglossus goldiei*), which breeds well on the colony system. The larger species are dangerous companions for other birds. They have been known to kill wild birds or those from adjoining aviaries that have been unfortunate enough to find their way into the enclosure.

In lories, behavior is not a reliable guide to sex. Two males or two females may be totally compatible and behave like a true pair. Sometimes two females will lay simultaneously, and only the appearance of four eggs indicates that the "pair" consists of two females! Chromosome sexing is recommended; many captive lories are overweight because of incorrect feeding and lack of exercise, and sex is difficult to determine surgically in obese birds.

Suspended aviaries, the most hygienic way of maintaining lories, may not provide sufficient protection from the elements in a cold climate. In this case, walk-in aviaries, with a concrete floor and a drain in the middle, are recommended. They can thus be hosed down daily. Alternatively, coarse gravel, to a depth of 15 cm (6 in), provides a surface that is easy to hose clean.

It is most important that lories have a nest box for roosting at all times. The wood should be thick, to provide extra warmth on cold nights and to withstand the extensive gnawing that occurs when the birds are breeding. Pieces of wood nailed inside, near the base, help the parents to keep the nest clean when chicks hatch. They gnaw at the wood to provide new nest litter.

If the nest is wet the chicks are almost certain to be plucked. The wood shavings used in the base of the nest must be changed as soon as they become damp; this might be as often as twice a week with large chicks. Holes drilled in the floor of the nest box allow some of the liquid feces to escape.

Nest hygiene is vitally important with lories. A damp nest may become a breeding ground for bacteria. Often the parents are blamed when chicks die, but their death could be due to bacterial infection. Between each clutch, the nest box should be emptied, sterilized and then filled to a depth of at least 5 cm (2 in) with clean shavings.

The most critical stage in the rearing period is when the female ceases to brood the chicks, before they are fully feathered. In Britain, for example, nearly all winter-hatched chicks die between six and ten days of age unless removed for hand-rearing after hatching.

Young lories that fledge into outdoor aviaries should be put back in the nest at night if the weather is cold or damp; otherwise they might not survive the night. Sometimes they refuse to remain within the nest, in which case they can be placed in a cardboard box, or a small darkened cage, and kept indoors overnight, to be returned to their parents early next morning.

There are several different genera of lories, the dietary requirements of which are discussed for each genus. However, they all consume "nectar", the ingredients of which are described under that heading.

See also: *Chalcopsitta*, *Charmosyna*, *Eos*, *Glossopsitta*, *Lorius*, *Neopsittacus*, *Oreopsittacus*, *Phigys*, *Pseudeos*, *Trichoglossus*, *Vini*.

Lorius LORIES

Highly intelligent and playful birds, these are the largest of the lories in body size. They have heavy bodies and medium-length wide tails. In all species, the beak is orange. The length of those birds known to aviculturists is 28–31 cm (11–12 in).

Remarks on care and feeding under *Chalcopsitta* Lories apply also to the members of this genus.

As is usual with lories, the clutch consists of two eggs, incubated by the female for about 25 days. The young spend about 10 to 11 weeks in the nest, but widely differing fledgling periods have been reported.

The best-known members of the

A Black-capped Lory (*Lorius lory lory*), aged 34 days.

genus are the Chattering Lory (*L. garrulus garrulus*) and a subspecies, which differs only in having yellow on the mantle, the Yellow-backed Lory (*L. g. flavopalliatus*). They are beautiful birds, scarlet with green wings and tail.

Less often available is the Black-capped Lory (*L. lory*), which differs from the Chattering Lory in having the forehead and crown black, a wide blue band on the mantle, and blue thighs and abdomen.

LOVEBIRDS (*Agapornis*)

Lovebirds are ideal subjects for beginners interested in breeding, or, more correctly, certain species, notably the Peach-faced, Masked and Fischer's are ideal. They are prolific, breed throughout the year, and do not need large cages. They can be bred indoors (see *CAGES*), but hatchability is usually better out of doors.

Feeding is simple: a mixture of canary, millet, and small sunflower seeds, and a little hemp in winter. Spray millet is a great favorite.

Parakeets (2)

A pair of Horned Parakeets *(Eunymphicus cornutus cornutus)* from New Caledonia.

Quaker Parakeets *(Myiopsitta monachus)* feeding on palm fruits – a favorite food of many parrots.

The female
Mustache Parakeet
*(Psittacula alexandri
fasciata)* is
distinguished by her
black upper
mandible.

Apple, diced carrot, and greens (seeding grasses, chickweed, spinach, etc.) are eaten, plus bread and milk when young are being reared. The more rarely kept Abyssinian needs more fruit.

Lovebirds originate from Africa (five species) and Madagascar (one species). The Black-collared (*A. swinderniana*) has never been kept alive in captivity, and the Abyssinian (*A. taranta*) and the Madagascar (*A. cana*) are not common, being difficult to breed in cold climates. Other species are firm favorites with thousands of breeders, most of whom keep the Peach-faced (*A. roseicollis*).

The Peach-faced lovebird is about 15 cm (6 in) in length; plumage is alike in male and female. The original wild type is green, with the face and throat salmon pink and the rump and tail coverts bright blue. Immature birds have softer colors, lack the red coloring on the forehead, and have brownish (not horn-colored) upper mandibles. Many mutations and their combinations are being bred. Young of several different colors can be produced in one nest.

Because the lovebird builds a nest (provide grasses, willow twigs, and fruit tree twigs for lovebirds to strip the bark), the nest box needs to be larger than usual for a bird of its size: it should measure approximately 23 × 15 × 17 cm high (9 × 6 × 7 in).

Females carry material into the nest tucked into the feathers of the rump; males do not usually do this. Another indication of sex is a clutch of ten eggs or more: a "pair" of two females laying simultaneously! The usual clutch size is about five and the incubation period 23 days. Newly hatched chicks have dark pink down. The young spend about six weeks in the nest, but will continue to be fed (mostly by the male) for some time, while the hen starts laying new eggs or looks for a new box.

The Masked Lovebird (*A. personata personata*) is unmistakable, with its black head and yellow breast; the wings are green. Immature birds are less brightly colored and have black at the base of the upper mandible. A conspicuous area of white skin surrounds the eye. Length is 15 cm (6 in). There is a very popular blue mutation, in which the green areas

are replaced by blue and the yellow by grayish-white. Breeding and management are as described for

the Peach-faced, except that colony breeding is not suitable.

The Black-cheeked Lovebird (*A. p. nigrigenis*) varies in availability; in Britain it is uncommon, yet in some European countries (Denmark, Germany, and the Netherlands, for example), many are bred. It is available in the U.S. It differs from the Masked Lovebird in having the top of the head brown, the upper breast a pale salmon color.

Fischer's Lovebird (*A. p. fischeri*) has the forehead, cheeks, and throat orange-red, upper breast and neck yellow, rump and uppertail coverts blue, and the tail tipped with lighter blue. The top of the head is smoky-brown. It is slightly smaller than the Masked Lovebird.

The Nyasa Lovebird (*A. p. lilianae*) differs from the Fischer's in lacking blue on the tail and rump and in its smaller size – 11 cm (4¼ in). There is a rare and extremely beautiful lutino mutation, which is pure yellow with the delicate pinkish-orange head color retained. The Nyasa breeds well on the colony system, but is rare in aviculture in most countries.

The Madagascar Lovebird (*A. cana*) can be sexed as soon as it feathers, the male having the head and breast gray, the upperparts dark green and the underparts light green. The beak is pale gray. The female is dark green above and slightly more yellowish-green below than the male. Length is 14 cm (5½ in).

Yellow Fischer's Lovebirds: the Fischer's, like the Masked and the Black-cheeked Lovebirds, have a white eye-ring.

M

MACAWS (*Ara*)

Because of their intelligence and individuality, macaws are among the most fascinating of aviary birds. Macaws include the largest and most spectacular members of the parrot family (see *HYACINTHINE MACAW* for members of the genus *Anodorhynchus*). Most macaws are included in the genus *Ara*, whose members vary greatly in coloration and size – from about 86 cm (34 in) to only 34 cm (13 in). Weight varies from well over 1,000 g (34 oz) in the Green-winged Macaw, to about 165 g (6 oz) in the smallest, the Hahn's. The feature that all the *Ara* species have in common is an area on the cheeks that is almost bare, being decorated with lines of tiny feathers in the larger species.

Undoubtedly many people have been drawn to parrot keeping by the desire to own a large macaw. Alas, these flamboyant birds have often attracted those with more money than sympathy. It is not unknown for wealthy people to choose a macaw to match the decor of their home!

Macaws are extremely sensitive birds; they need to be with their own kind, but if kept alone as a pet, it is essential that they are among those who understand them. If not, their lives are miserable and they develop unfortunate habits, such as screaming or plucking themselves.

In any case, keeping a large macaw in a home creates many problems. These birds are extremely noisy, with far-carrying voices. It is impossible to keep one without damage to furniture or furnishings, so the house-proud, and those with close neighbors or intolerant family members can rule out the idea of a pet macaw. So can those who do not spend much time at home. Macaws are simply too demanding for the average person to cope with.

Except for the very fortunate minority who are able to keep macaws at liberty, the only practical method is housing them in an aviary. Suspended or traditional types of cages can be used – and the larger the better. Many macaws kept in aviaries do not attempt to fly because the enclosure is simply too small. It is thrilling to see a macaw in flight, even if only over a short distance. A flight area 8 m (26 ft) long is therefore recommended for the large species.

Regrettably, many breeding pairs are kept in enclosures so small that the birds have no opportunity to exercise their wings. This practice will eventually lead to very poor specimens being produced. Macaws *must* be able to exercise their wings fully. The need to do so is evident at an early age – in young birds being hand-reared at weaning stage, for example. When removed from their cage they flap their wings vigorously for a long time; other parrots also do this, but for a few seconds only.

The large macaws are truly omnivorous and will consume a wide range of foods. They have a need for hard foods such as nuts (especially Brazils, walnuts, and raw coconut) and can also be given pebbles to grind and play with. Seeds and the smaller nuts, such as peanuts and pine nuts, should form no more than 50% of the diet. Seeds can include sunflower, safflower, buckwheat, oats or groats, wheat and hemp, and also spray millet. Fresh fruit and vegetables, as well as cooked beans and other cooked vegetables should form about 30% of the diet. The larger species should be offered animal protein to stimulate breeding and when young are in the nest. A chop bone or cooked chicken carcass is especially relished.

The small macaws, often known as dwarf macaws, have less need for animal protein. Their nuts need to be cracked or halved and canary seed and millet can be added to their seed mixture.

Macaws are impossible to sex by outward appearance, and surgical or chromosome sexing is recommended. Possibly more same-sex "pairs" have been kept together by owners convinced that they had a true pair of macaws than in any other group of parrots. A strange phenomenon in three species is the imbalance in the sex ratio: by far the majority of Scarlet Macaws in captivity are males;

A male Uvaeen
Parakeet
*(Eunymphicus
cornutus uvaeensis)* a
highly endangered
species with a very
small habitat.

Parakeets (3)

A Port Lincoln Parakeet *(Barnadius zonarius zonarius).*

An Amboina King Parakeet *(Alisterus amboinensis amboinensis)* from the islands of Amboina and Ceram in Indonesia.

The male Alexandrine Parakeet *(Psittacula eupatria)* has an enormously long tail. A single feather can measure as much as 36 cm (14 in).

there are more Green-winged males than females, and in the Blue and Yellow Macaw, females predominate.

This explains why there are so many couples consisting of a male Scarlet and a female Blue and Yellow and is one reason why so many hybrid macaws are reared. In the United States, hybrids are popular, and may even sell for more than pure species, and so the various crosses have been given different names. Hybridizing, however, unless there is a very good reason for it, is to be condemned, especially in the case of the large macaws because they are endangered in the wild.

Compatibility is of extreme importance in breeding macaws: owning a male and a female of the same species is not enough. If the birds do not like each other, it is a waste of time persevering. Although I condemn hybrid breeding, it must be admitted that often a large macaw will fall instantly in love with a bird of another species, and then the owner does not have the heart to part the devoted couple. Such situations are best avoided.

The large macaws can be dangerously aggressive when breeding. The nest box should therefore be situated where it can be inspected from outside the aviary. A barrel on its side can be used as a nest site, but it should not be too large. It is best mounted outside the aviary for ease of inspection.

When macaws become noisier and more aggressive than usual, breeding can be expected. The clutch size in the large species (Red-fronted Macaw and upwards in size) is two to four eggs, and the incubation period is 24 to 28 days. Incubation is carried out by the female, but many males spend long periods inside the nest. The young fledge after about 90 to 95 days, but there is considerable variation in this period.

Many macaws are excellent parents and look after their young perfectly. Rearing from the egg by the breeder is not recommended except in an emergency. If the parents refuse to feed the young, I prefer to arrange their foster care by other macaws or even *Aratinga* conures. The only disadvantage of parent-reared chicks is that they

are much more difficult to tame. However, if placed in a small aviary when they are independent and can be removed from their parents, most will become tame after a few weeks.

All macaws should be provided with a rearing food when chicks are in the nest. This can consist of a commercial food with the addition of hard-boiled egg, or a mixture of whole wheat bread with grated carrot, chopped greens, hard-boiled egg, and a little peanut butter, for example.

A cooked rearing food, used with success by one breeder, consisted of four cups each of chicken scratch feed and rice and eight cups of water, cooked for about 45 minutes. To this was added ¼ cup of corn syrup, six cups of parrot mixture, and 450 g (1 lb) each of sweetcorn and frozen mixed vegetables. Sometimes four cups of dog food or monkey chow were added, plus brewer's yeast, bone meal, cod liver oil, and vitamins. This quantity fed ten macaws for three or four days.

Macaws enjoy bread, biscuits, fresh corn on the cob (an excellent weaning food), and a wide variety of items from the table, cooked and uncooked.

The large *Ara* species most likely to be encountered are the Blue-and-Yellow (*A. ararauna*), Green-winged (*A. chloroptera*) and the Scarlet (*A. macao*). The first, often known as the Blue-and-Gold, is mainly rich sky blue above and yellow below. The length, including the long tail (about half the total) is about 85 cm (33 in). This is one of the most free-breeding macaws and can be recommended to those who have not previously kept large macaws. It is the most numerous in captivity and one of the most plentiful in the wild. It occurs throughout tropical South America and Panama.

Approximately the same area of distribution is shared by the Green-winged Macaw; it is about the same total length but considerably larger in body size and greater in weight. It has the most massive head and bill of any macaw except the Hyacinthine. Plumage is mainly crimson on the head and underparts, dark green on the wings, and light blue on the back, rump and tail coverts. This is an underrated species that has never achieved the popularity of the now much more expensive Scarlet.

The Scarlet is often considered to be the most beautiful member of the genus, with its fiery scarlet plumage set off by the yellow on the center of the wing and the light sky-blue back, rump, and upper tail coverts. The facial skin is bare of markings. In length it is about 90 cm (35 in).

In all the large macaws, young birds can be distinguished by the indistinct grayish color of the iris of the eye, lighter coloration of the beak, and, on fledging, by the shorter tail.

The Military Macaw (*Ara militaris mexicana*) from Mexico has dense, short red feathers on the forehead, its chin is brown, and its rump and upper tail coverts are light blue. The tail feathers are maroon, tipped with blue above. The plumage is otherwise mainly olive green. In length it is about 70 cm (27 in).

Buffon's Macaw (*A. ambigua*) reaches a length of 82 cm (32 in). The upper side of the tail is more orange-red than maroon.

Both these macaws have the bare skin on their faces, decorated with lines of tiny red and blackish-brown feathers. The sheer size of Buffon's Macaws makes them imposing birds. The Military, seldom kept as a pet, is an extremely attractive aviary bird.

There are six small species of *Ara* macaws that are often given the name of dwarf macaws. They make enchanting pets, especially if hand-reared, being highly intelligent, playful, and affectionate. They will also learn to mimic a few words. Their voices are loud and harsh and they are, of course, destructive, but the smallest, such as the Hahn's, can be highly recommended as pets, if obtained when young.

As aviary birds dwarf macaws are delightful, being hardy (with the exception of the Red-bellied, *A. manilata*), inquisitive, and often extremely free-breeding. I know of a pair of Illiger's (*A. maracana*) in England that reared 79 young between February, 1978, when obtained, and April, 1986, when I last heard from their owner! These young were parent-reared.

The small macaws generally lay three or four eggs that are incubated by the female for between 24 and 26 days. The young spend 13 or 14 weeks in the nest.

The dwarf macaws consist of the following species: Yellow-collared, also called Yellow-naped (*A. auricollis*), which measures about 40 cm (16 in); Severe Macaw (*A. severa*), also called Chestnut-fronted Macaw, which is 49 cm (19 in) long; Hahn's (*A. nobilis nobilis*) and the Noble Macaw (*A. n. cumanensis*). One species, Coulon's (*A. couloni*) is unknown in captivity, and the Red-bellied is extremely susceptible to stress and recommended only for the most experienced macaw keepers.

Micropsitta – see *PYGMY PARROTS*

MOLTING

Parrots normally molt once a year, each individual usually molting at about the same time each year. Stress or shock can bring on a partial or premature molt. In a severe case of shock, most of the flight feathers could be molted in a few hours, or a partial molt of various feathers could occur. Normally, the molt is a gradual process; only one or two flight feathers are molted at the same time, so that the bird's flight capability is not impaired.

Dishonest persons, attempting to sell a parrot that has plucked itself, or one that is suffering from Psittacine Beak and Feather Disease Syndrome, may claim that the bird is molting, but under normal circumstances there is little apparent loss of feather during this process. Molt is more obvious in birds that have a number of head feathers in quills because they have no companion to preen their head feathers, or because they belong to a species in which mutual preening does not occur. Missing flight feathers may be noticed when the wing is stretched. Otherwise than in these circumstances the molt should not be conspicuous.

The duration of the molt varies according to the individual and species. Some of the larger parrots can take two months to molt completely, apart from the flight feathers, which are renewed over a much longer period. Not all the flight feathers are renewed every year, so it may be two years before

Macaws

Hahn's Macaw *(Ara nobilis nobilis)*, the smallest of the macaws, measures only 34 cm (13 in).

Hyacinthine Macaws *(Anodorhynchus hyacinthinus)* – the largest and one of the most magnificent of parrot species.

Blue and Yellow Macaws *(Ara ararauna)* are the most commonly kept and bred of the large *Ara* species.

The Green-winged Macaw *(Ara chloroptera)* is perhaps the most underrated of the large macaws.

N and O

a parrot received with cut wings has grown every feather. Pet owners who clip their birds' wings must check the state of regrowth. It could happen that the bird will molt soon after clipping, and the owner may be unprepared for the fact that very soon it will again be capable of flight.

Birds that are molting need moisture on their plumage even more than at other times of year. Owners should be sure to spray their pet birds with warm water, every day if possible. The growing feather is encased in a whitish sheath that can become quite hard without moisture.

This protective sheath gradually disintegrates. Occasionally, however, it fails to do so, and then it hardens and prevents the feather from opening. When this occurs on a tail or flight feather, the sheath should be softened with warm water and gently removed. Unless this is done soon after the sheath should have normally disintegrated, the feather will be useless. If several feathers are affected in this way, it is usually an indication that the bird is in poor condition. A vitamin and mineral supplement should then be added to a favorite item of food two or three times a week for several weeks to try to correct any deficiency in the diet.

It is natural for a bird to scratch frequently when molting and to preen vigorously, thus releasing a considerable amount of feather debris and dead skin. Also renewed about once a year is the skin on the feet, and the skin to which the contour feathers are attached.

The age at which the first molt occurs varies according to the species. In small species, it may be only a few weeks after they have fledged; in larger parrots, such as Amazons and macaws, the first molt occurs at the age of about nine or ten months. However, the time of year when the bird hatched may influence this.

Feathers are composed of protein, and increasing the amount of protein in the diet or giving animal protein before and during the molt, must aid the production of good quality feather. (See *PROTEIN, ANIMAL.*)

Nandayus CONURE

The reason that the single member of this genus, the Nanday Conure (*Nandayus nenday*), has been separated from the *Aratinga* conures is not clear. Its care and breeding are the same as recommended for the members of the *Aratinga* genus.

This species is identified by its black head and black beak. In length it is about 31 cm (12 in). The throat and upper breast are blue and the thighs are red.

It originates from Brazil, Bolivia, Paraguay, and northern Argentina, where it occurs in large flocks.

This species has a reputation for being very noisy. However, it is very free-breeding, and the hand-reared young are much quieter and make delightful and affectionate pets.

Nannopsittaca PARROTLETS

This genus contains two species, one of which was discovered as recently as October, 1985. While working in the Manu National Park in Peru, Dr Charles A. Munn observed a small parrotlet that he was unable to identify – five individuals in all. The following year he repeatedly observed flocks of the same species at a location 30 km (18½ mi) further downstream. This species has since been observed by other ornithologists in an unexplored region east of the Peruvian city of Pucallpa, near the Brazilian border. Still unnamed, it appears to belong in this genus, being bright green, with powder-blue forecrown, flesh-colored bill and feet, and a faint light iris of the eye.

The Tepui Parrotlet (*N. panychlora*) is all green, except for yellow around the eye, especially under it. The tail is short and square, the bill is dusky and the iris is brown. Length is about 14 cm (5½ in). This species originates from southern Venezuela, in the Pantepui region, adjacent to extreme western Guyana. It occurs only on the summits and slopes of isolated mountains and most of its habitat is inaccessible, which accounts for its being totally unknown in aviculture. It is apparently not rare, being seen in large flocks in the only part of its range that is easily accessible.

A flock was encountered by a Guyanese explorer making an unsuccessful attempt to scale the precipitous face of a mountain in the Pacaraima range. Base camp was establshed at 2,100 m (6,900 ft); above it the mountain rose sheer for 540 m (1,800 ft) to the summit. Here every morning and evening the flock could be heard moving to and from their feeding grounds in the forest below. Their flights took them through the cumulus cloud level. Almost continuous mist and cloud prevented the observers from actually seeing the birds which, it was believed, could have numbered several thousands.

Assuming that the new species is a *Nannopsittaca*, this genus is the least known of all neotropical parrots.

NECTAR

Many different ingredients can form nectar – the liquid food given to lories. The basis is usually baby cereal and honey or glucose, plus, except in a warm climate, a little baby milk formula or condensed milk. One can purchase nectar mixtures in powder form. Several kinds are excellent, but they tend to be expensive and therefore out of the question for most people who keep more than half a dozen lories. For this reason, most breeders make up their own mixture. The consistency should be runny and the ingredients should not be too rich; large quantities of milk and cereal could result in overweight birds and fatty degeneration of the liver.

The mixture I have used for many years is made as follows: approximately one large tablespoon of malt extract and 1 oz of honey (or glucose) are dissolved in about 15 fluid oz) of hot boiled water. Then 2–3 tablespoonfuls of baby cereal are added and stirred, and hot and cold water added to make about 70 fluid oz of nectar. The mixture is fed warm because this is how lories prefer it! Various fruits, or carrot, liquefied in a blender, are added on occasion, and more rarely also a vitamin and mineral supplement.

Other items that can be used are malted drinks, invalid foods, baby rice (dry form), wheat germ cereal (if made into a flour in a blender), and jars of apple sauce or fruit dessert baby foods bought in jars and cans.

Most nectar separates after a few hours, so this should be fed twice daily. There is a move now towards feeding lories mainly on dry foods. However, some species could not exist on such a diet, and until the long-term effects of this are known, I would hesitate to recommend it.

Neophema PARAKEETS – see *GRASS PARAKEETS*

Neopsittacus LORIES

The two small lorikeets that comprise this genus come from New Guinea. Unusual among lories, they have, on the underparts, a shade of red that one associates with neotropical parrots rather than lories – a dark red like a Green-winged Macaw. The beak is extremely strong, indicating that in the wild they feed on seed more extensively than other lories. In captivity, seed should form at least 50% of the diet.

Musschenbroek's Lorikeet (*N. musschenbroekii*) measures 23 cm (9 in). The head is green, streaked with yellow, and the crown and nape are brown (browner in the male). The underparts are irregularly marked with red, and the underside of the tail is orange-yellow, with yellow at the tip. The beak is orange and the eye red. Immature birds have only a tinge of red on their underparts.

This species was almost unknown in aviculture until the late 1970s; no commercial importations reached Britain until 1986. By this time, they had been bred in Germany and Denmark, but were not well established. Most of the birds available to date have been wild-caught and are very nervous. Unlike most lories, they seem to take a long time to settle down in captivity. They are rarely available in the U.S.

The diet should consist of a mixture of small seeds, such as groats, hemp, white millet, and canary seeds; they will also eat rice, pumpkin seeds, and small pine nuts. Millet spray should be given frequently, preferably daily, as this is greatly relished. Their very strong beaks can even deal with walnuts in slightly cracked shells! (I had mine a year before I discovered their liking for these.) They also like corn on the cob, sweet corn kernels, carrot, apple, soaked figs, orange, soaked raisins, and soaked sunflower seeds. If offered a suitably varied diet, these lories will consume only a small amount of nectar.

For their size, they have perhaps more powerful beaks than any other parrot. At all costs, avoid being bitten by a Musschenbroek's Lorikeet! They are extremely destructive to woodwork and should be provided with fresh branches for gnawing at least once a week. They are also adept at opening doors that are not properly secured.

The clutch size is two eggs, incubated for about 24 days by the female.

The Alpine or Emerald Lorikeet (*N. pullicauda*) differs from Musschenbroek's in its smaller size, being 18 cm (7 in). It also has a more extensive area of red on the breast, and the nape is only tinged with brown. Occasionally a single bird of this species has been found in a consignment of Musschenbroek's. Lory enthusiasts are ever on the lookout for them, as they are extremely rare in captivity.

NEST BOXES

Nest boxes should be constructed of wood, not of metal or a material such as plastic. It is true that plastic would be easy to keep clean, but breeding parrots must be able to gnaw at the inside of their nest. Initially, this nest preparation stimulates egg-laying. The interior is gnawed away to provide a suitable surface for the eggs. When the chicks hatch, the wood chips gnawed from the interior of the nest assist in keeping it dry and sanitary.

The feces of the chicks are not, of course, removed from the nest in hole-nesting birds, and thus fresh wood shavings must be added. Better still, pieces of wood should be screwed on inside the box; this prolongs the life of the box (an important consideration in view of the high cost of wood), reduces the likelihood of accidents as a result of the base of the nest

being destroyed, and prevents the breeder's having to change or repair a nest that contains eggs or young.

The wood chosen must be waterproof; marine plywood is a good choice.

Metal is totally unsuitable for nesting sites. Despite this, some breeders do use metal waste containers for large destructive birds such as cockatoos. This is to be deplored; metal becomes unacceptably hot in summer and very cold in winter. Many parrots nest in the winter or use their box for roosting, so it must be cozy inside. The box should be of wood lined with welded mesh; inside,

The nest-box must be situated where it can be inspected without entering the aviary.

large pieces of wood should be screwed on (not nailed, as projecting nails could cause serious injury).

To make the nest box waterproof, roofing felt can be nailed to the top of the boxes of less destructive species. All nest boxes should be placed where they are well shielded from the weather, if necessary by protecting the area with heavy plastic sheeting. By far the best site for the nest box is outside the aviary, but inside a covered passage, where the nest can be inspected in complete safety, regardless of the weather.

Except in a very shallow nest box, it is essential to have a ladder leading from the nest entrance to the base. This can be made from wire or from wood – both have serious disadvantages and advantages. Several pieces of wood nailed horizontally are safest, provided that the nest is regularly inspected; these ladder rungs could be gnawed away, leaving a bird trapped inside. The other alternative is a ladder of welded mesh; it should be bent so that it bows out slightly, thus reducing the risk of a bird's being trapped by its own nails – a horrible fate. Every effort must be made to avoid this.

Given a choice, most parrots will choose smaller nests than those that breeders usually provide. In the wild, spacious nests are seldom available; indeed some are so small that, as the young grow, they have to stand on top of each other. As a general guide, the nest box should be slightly longer than the length of the bird's body, minus its tail.

There are exceptions: the lovebird species, which carry material inside and build a bulky nest, need a box of twice this capacity. Also, birds known to lay very large clutches (such as some Rosellas, parrotlets, and certain *Pyrrhura* conures) will also need a more spacious nest.

Some examples of nest box sizes are as follows:

cockatiel, 20 cm (8 in) square and 31 cm (12 in) high;

Grass Parakeets (*Neophemas*), 18 cm (7 in) square and 31 cm (12 in) high;

Ringneck and similar-sized *Psittacula* Parakeets, 25 cm (10 in) square and 61 cm (2 ft) high;

Kakarikis, 20 cm (8 in) square and 31 cm (12 in) high;

Rosellas (*Platycercus*), 23 cm (9 in) square and 60 cm (2 ft) to 1.2 m (4 ft) high;

Goldie's Lorikeet, 13 cm (5 in) square and 23 cm (9 in) high;

Chattering Lory and Blue-fronted Amazon, 25 cm (10 in) square and 61 cm (2 ft) high;

Blue and Yellow Macaw, (horizontal) 39 cm (15 in) square and 105 cm (41 in) long.

Measurements given are internal dimensions.

The nest entrance should be only large enough to admit the species. If the opening is too large, there will be too much light inside. The entrance does not have to be round or centrally positioned. Anyone who possesses a saw, but not a drill, will find that a square entrance hole in the corner of the nest is just as acceptable to the birds; indeed, they probably prefer it, as one corner of the nest will always be in darkness.

For nest inspection, bear in mind that birds panic when a hand approaches them from above, cutting off their only means of escape. Inspection should be via a hinged flap in the side. Do not make this flap tight-fitting, or when the wood becomes damp it will expand. Be sure there is a secure and easily operated catch to keep the flap closed; use a padlock where there is any opportunity for theft.

The perch below the nest entrance can be made from a dowel or from a short piece of natural wood (from fruit trees, ash, maple, poplar, etc.). The perch should extend a little way inside the nest, as many males like to sit at the entrance when their females are incubating.

Wood shavings, or a mixture of this material and peat, are suitable for the base of the box. Be careful about the source of the wood shavings: those obtained from a lumberyard may contain wood that has been treated with a preservative that is harmful to birds. The best source is the packed litter sold in pet shops.

The position of the nest box will depend on a number of factors, such as prevailing winds and the need for a sheltered location. For birds that breed in spring and summer, it is usually best to place the box in the outside flight area

Nest sites for macaws, such as this barrel, should be mounted outside the aviary for ease of inspection.

with immediate overhead cover. For some winter breeders, such as lovebirds, it may be best to place the box in the shelter, but bear in mind that hatchability may be higher in an outdoor location.

For aggressive birds, those that are nervous, and for females who rush back to the nest before one can reach it, the nest box must be positioned to coincide with an inspection door in the side of the aviary, or it must open on to a service passage. If nest inspection is difficult, breeding results will be poor. It is essential to know what is happening within the nest.

Barrels are sometimes used as nests for cockatoos and macaws. The disadvantage is that it is difficult to position barrels in such a way that nest inspection can occur from outside the aviary, unless they are built into the side of the enclosure when it is first constructed.

For seasonal breeders and those that do not roost in their boxes, the nest boxes should be removed or boarded up out of the breeding season. Their renewed availability acts as a stimulus to breeding.

NEST SITES IN THE WILD

It is well known that the majority of parrots nest in holes in trees, but there are some interesting exceptions. This depends more on the locality of the bird than on the species. An excellent example is the Bahaman Amazon Parrot (*Amazona leucocephala bahamensis*), a race of the Cuban Amazon. It is now confined to two islands.

On Inagua it nests in trees, but on Abaco the only trees are pines and most are too small for nest sites. Here, therefore, the parrots use underground cavities in limestone rocks.

A number of species of macaws, Amazons, and conures nest in holes in rock faces. In captivity, many macaws choose to nest on the ground. Unusual nest sites chosen by Amazons in the wild include the stone wall of an ancient Mayan temple in Guatemala and an old chimney on the island of St. Vincent in the Caribbean.

Parrots in Australia, Africa, and South and Central America – have discovered what useful nesting sites are termitaria – the homes of termites. In Central America, the Half-moon Conure (*Aratinga canicularis*) is so dependent on these sites that distribution of this conure is directly related to that of the termites. After hollowing out their nest in the termitarium, the conures desert it until the termites have sealed up the entrances from the tunnels leading to the conures' chamber.

Not only are termitaria easily excavated sites, but the termites offer protection against nest predators. Most termite nests are situated in trees, but they may also be built on the ground. In Australia huge free-standing termitaria, in the tropical Cape York region, harbor nests of the Golden-shouldered Parakeet (also known as the Anthill Parrot). Because of the high temperature within during the day the female does not incubate for several daytime hours and also leaves the young unbrooded. Aviary-breeding of this species therefore presents a unique problem that has been overcome by providing electrically heated nest boxes.

In Africa, the little Red-faced Lovebird (*Agapornis pullaria*) uses termitaria in trees and on the ground. This species has very rarely been bred in captivity, but success has occurred using a specially constructed bale of peat or nest box packed with peat to simulate a termitarium.

Other lovebird species are very much less specialized in their nesting requirements. The Peach-faced, for example, has been known to use crevices in buildings and, more commonly, to take over weavers' nests. Among the most prolific birds in the world, weavers breed in colonies containing thousands, or hundreds of thousands of nests.

In the neotropics small parrots in arid localities, in which trees are scarce or nonexistent, nest in cacti. A correspondent in Argentina once described nests of the little Aymara Parakeet (*Bolborhynchus aymara*), located within a cactus, surrounded by low spiny bushes, "a truly impenetrable combination." Another member of the same genus from Argentina, the Mountain Parakeet (*B. aurifrons*), has been known to form a nest by burrowing into an earth bank. In captivity, this species will use an ordinary nest box.

Two of the best-known parrots that do not use holes in trees are the Quaker Parakeet and the Patagonian Conure.

Little is known of the nesting habits of lories outside Australia. Thane Pratt, of the Department of Biology at Rutgers University, made some interesting observations on this subject. After noticing certain small species in New Guinea exploring the thick moss "cushions" draped over tree limbs in the forest canopy, he continued to watch with interest. He saw Fairy Lorikeets climbing into one of these cushions, which may be several feet thick and support small "gardens" of orchids and ferns. Josephine's Lorikeets were also seen leaving a clump of epiphytes from which chicks were heard calling.

According to people of the Huon Peninsula of New Guinea, Papuan Lorikeets choose to nest in the massive accumulations of dead leaves in the crowns of *Pandanus* palms. In captivity, all small lorikeets readily accept a nest box, except the Goldie's, many of which are reluctant to enter a box.

Little is known of the nesting habits of many species of parrots, but it is clear that their nest sites are not necessarily holes in trees!

NET

A net for catching birds is essential equipment for those who keep birds in aviaries or suspended cages. The net should be one designed for the purpose – not a fish net, for example. The bird net should have a padded rim to prevent possible injury to the bird and the material must be suitable. Cotton is best, not nylon or a mesh in which the bird's claws could become entangled. The material should be a neutral color or a dark one, such as brown, not white or a bright shade.

Anyone who keeps parrot species ranging from the largest to the smallest should have nets of three different sizes, the diameters being approximately 18 cm (7 in), 25 cm (10 in), and 36 cm (14 in). Because of the difficulty in catching birds in suspended cages, nets with extra long handles are necessary.

It is generally easier and quicker to catch a bird when it is flying, because when it is clinging to the wire one has the additional task of releasing beak and feet. To avoid being bitten through the net, grasp the bird's head with thumb and forefinger on either side of the mandibles so that it cannot maneuver its head to bite. The claws can then be released.

Always keep the catching nets in good repair and in the same place, so that in an emergency you do not have to search for them.

NIGHT PARROT (*Geopsittacus occidentalis*)

Nocturnal and almost certainly nomadic, the Night Parrot has been described as the most mysterious of Australian birds. Only one specimen (no longer in existence) has been collected this century, and there are only two reliable reports of its having been seen. Found only in the Australian interior, it must have declined greatly, and may already be extinct in the eastern part of its range, from which there have been no records for more than 60 years.

Great was the excitement in June, 1979, therefore, when four birds were sighted at Coopers Creek in far northeastern South Australia. This occurred in a vast area of undisturbed habitat. One bird was flushed by approaching camels, rising up about 30 m (100 ft) in front of the camels and flying 4 or 5 m (13–16 ft) close to the ground. Then people on foot disturbed three more birds at the base of a bush. They flew at a height of 3–4 m (10–13 ft) before dropping down into dense vegetation.

What a wonderful moment it must have been for the ornithologists, who sighted these birds – to have proof at last that the species still survived.

The Night Parrot is small, about 23 cm (9 in) long, with a short, gradated tail. It is yellowish-green, mottled with brown, black, and yellow. The bill is horn-colored and the iris is black. It is closely associated with spinifex (*Triodia*). *The Atlas of Australian Birds* states: "A study of the records in South Australia concludes that samphire flats associated with lake systems may be important to the survival of the Night Parrot, perhaps specially between years of heavy rain; when rain brings the spinifex into flower and the seeds ripen, the parrot may move out from the lakes to the spinifex sandplains."

There is only one credible record of this species in captivity. A single bird, caught in South Australia in 1867, was sent to the London Zoo. The parrot survived for four months, apparently dying of pneumonia in January, 1868. In that era most parrots were kept in hothouse conditions, so it is surprising that it was apparently kept out of doors. Never again is this little-known bird likely to be seen outside Australia.

Ognorhynchus PARROT
Little is known about the single member of this genus, the Yellow-eared Parrot (*O. icterotis*), which has also been called a conure or parakeet. In my opinion, it is most closely allied to the macaws. Its large bill and habit of "blushing" are macawlike, as is its general behavior. In size and silhouette it is similar to the Thick-billed Parrot (*Rhynchopsitta*).

Its coloration is distinctive. The forehead, part of the crown, ear coverts, and part of the cheeks are bright yellow. The tail is green above, dull maroon on the inner webs, and pale maroon on the underside. The rest of the plumage is green, darker above, and more yellowish-green below. The beak is black, as is the bare skin surrounding the eye. In length it is about 41 cm (16 in).

This species occurs only in the Andes of southwestern Colombia and adjacent northern Ecuador, mainly between 2,300 and 3,000 m (7,550–9,850 ft). Regrettably, much of its former habitat has been deforested in recent years. A substantial population decline must have occurred, but this parrot has rarely been observed – let alone studied – so no population estimate is available. Much of its believed range in Ecuador is almost inaccessible, so an undisturbed population may survive there.

The Yellow-eared Parrot is extremely rare in captivity. The only substantiated reports are of two birds received by a London dealer, on separate occasions, in 1965. One of these was later presented to Vogelpark Walsrode in Germany, after the owner had made repeated unsuccessful attempts to purchase the other.

Opopsitta – see under *FIG PARROTS*

Oreopsittacus LORIKEET
The single member of this genus, the Alpine Lorikeet (*O. arfaki*), is unknown in aviculture. It has been collected on several occasions, but has proved impossible to keep alive for more than a few days. Thus it seems that this tiny parrot (15 cm/ 6 in) is unlikely to be available to collectors.

It is exquisitely and unusually colored. The male has a red forehead and crown, and purple lores and cheeks, with two rows of white dots, or streaks, below the eye. His abdomen and lower flanks are yellow, red, or green, and the underwing coverts and sides of the breast are red. The tail is green above and rose-red below. The plumage is otherwise mainly green.

The female has a green crown and forehead.

Uniquely among parrots, this lorikeet has 14 tail feathers (instead of 12).

Found in the mountains of New Guinea, it has been observed there in small groups.

P

PALM COCKATOO – see under
BLACK COCKATOOS

PARROTLETS (*Forpus*)

Members of this genus are the
smallest parrots known in
aviculture, being smaller, on
average, than the lovebirds, their
African counterparts. The smallest
of the genus, the Spectacled
Parrotlet (*F. conspicillatus*)
measures only 11 cm (4⅓ in), and
the largest, the Yellow-faced (*F.
xanthops*), has a total length of 19
cm (7½ in). All have very short
tails.

They are basically light green,
the males having blue on the rump
and/or wings. The females of some
species are difficult to distinguish.

They originate in South and
Central America. There are seven
species: the Celestial (or Pacific),
Yellow-faced, Spectacled,
Blue-winged, Mexican, Guiana (or
Green-rumped) and Solater's.

Parrotlets have many factors in
their favor. Being so small they are
inexpensive to feed and to house.
They are extremely quiet. They
nest readily and breed at a very
early age. The only major problem
with these little birds is that, if
closely confined, one bird may kill
another. Males may also act
aggressively towards young males
after fledging, and therefore these
youngsters should be removed soon
after they are able to feed
themselves properly. This can be as
soon as ten days after leaving the
nest.

Many parrotlets eat only seed,
but will sample bread and milk
when their chicks hatch. Their
staple diet should consist of the
usual range of small seeds (canary,
millet, groats, hemp, and small
sunflower seeds); fruit should also
be offered. Those at Loro Parque
relish the small orange fruits from
the palm trees there, which have a
fibrous exterior; they cannot eat
the hard nut in the center. Other
foods sampled by parrotlets have
included spinach, seeding
forget-me-nots, moistened sponge
cake, and granola cereal (oats,
wheat flakes, raisins, chopped nuts,
and dates). Sprouted seed should
be given to those that will take only
seed.

A suitable nest box would
measure about 18 cm (7 in) square
and 20 cm (8 in) high. Four to six
eggs are laid and incubated by the
female for about 20 to 23 days.
Chicks have white down that is
fairly sparse. A distinctive feature
is the bill coloration, which is
mainly deep pink.

Forpus chicks have the great
asset of being sexable as soon as
they feather up, at about three
weeks of age. They will consume
spray millet from the age of five or
six weeks and are independent by
eight weeks. They spend five weeks
in the nest.

PARROTLETS (*Touit*) – see
TOUIT PARROTLETS

PATAGONIAN CONURE
(*Cyanoliseus patagonus*)

This large, very sociable, and
distinctively colored conure (which
has a feathered cere) is the only
member of the genus. There are
three subspecies, of which only the
Lesser Conure (*C. p. patagonus*)
from Argentina is well known in
aviculture. The head, upperparts
and most of the breast are
olive-green; the abdomen and
thighs are olive-brown, red, and
yellow; the rump and tail coverts
are yellow. Its length is 43–46 cm
(17–18 in).

The much rarer Greater Conure
(*C. p. byroni*), from central Chile,
which measures about 53 cm (20½
in), usually has a broken band of
white on the upper breast (the
Lesser Conure has a little white at
the sides of the neck).

The Andean Patagonian Conure
(*C. p. andinus*), from southwestern
Argentina, has little or no yellow
on the abdomen, less red, and

Yellow-faced
Parrotlets and other
Forpus species can
be sexed as soon as
the feathers erupt.

lacks the white near the neck.

The extremely loud and far-carrying voice of this conure rules it out of many collections. This is regrettable, because it is a most attractive bird and breeds well in aviaries. Colony breeding is sometimes carried out but this is not recommended, as only the dominant pair may breed. On the other hand, keeping two pairs in one aviary apears to be a good arrangement.

At Loro Parque two pairs share the same enclosure nest simultaneously and do an excellent job of rearing the young. The clutch usually consists of three to five eggs, which are incubated for 24 or 25 days. The young leave the nest at eight weeks. Obtained as soon as they are independent, they make the most delightful and affectionate pets, their loud voices being their only drawback.

The diet should be as recommended for *Pionus* parrots.

The people of Argentina often call this bird the "bank-burrowing" parrot because it burrows up to 1.5 m (5 ft) deep into the side of a cliff or a bank to nest.

PESQUET'S PARROT (*Psittrichas fulgidus*)

This species is one of the most distinctive and aberrant of the parrots. A native of New Guinea, it is a fascinating bird, its large size and red and black plumage rendering it unmistakable.

It has a peculiar head (small and partly bare of feathers) and bill (elongated). Both these features must be adaptations for feeding on fruit. In captivity it is very noticeable that no seed or other hard foods are consumed, the hardest item being whole carrots. Fruit should not be cut into small pieces; instead, half a pear, half a banana, and a large piece of papaya (a great favorite), for example, should be spiked onto a nail. Most fruits can be offered. One breeder made a porridge consisting of diced fruits, rolled oats, rice flour, breakfast cereals, milk powder, honey, calcium and vitamins.

Pairs rearing young must be offered protein; ground horse meat and hard-boiled egg have been found acceptable. However, a chick that hatched at Loro Parque in my absence was reared for the

first two weeks on nothing more than fruit, carrot, and bread and milk. It was then removed for hand-rearing. It differed from parrot chicks of other species in its manner of gaping for food like a softbill. It was fed on the same food as other large parrots being hand-reared at the time, but its feces were entirely different, being soft and cream-colored. This proves that the digestive system is entirely different from that of omnivorous and seed-eating parrots.

Very intelligent and aware of its surroundings, it was a fascinating chick to rear and never gave any problems. At about 75 days, it started to sample soft foods, including papaya and fresh corn on the cob.

This species lays two eggs at intervals of three or four days. The female incubates for 29 or 30 days. The young spend about 15 weeks in the nest. At Loro Parque, nesting was stimulated by providing a palm

A Pesquet's Parrot aged about 84 days. Note the natal down still adhering to the feathers of crown and nape, and the hairlike feathers on cheeks and ear coverts.

A Pesquet's Parrot (*Psittrichas fulgidus*), hand-reared at Loro Parque, aged about 55 days.

log in which an entrance hole, about 10 cm (4 in) in depth, had been made. The male did most, or all, of the excavation, to a depth of about 1.2 m (4 ft), carrying out the excavated material in his plumage, so that every day there would be a pile on the ground near the log.

It is generally accepted that this species is sexually dimorphic; males have a few red feathers behind the eye. It appears, however, that young birds of both sexes show this color, as has at least one adult female on record.

Pesquet's Parrots, although hardy in the sense that they tolerate cold weather, are extremely sensitive to change. Moving them to a new aviary should be avoided unless absolutely necessary. They are also susceptible to candidiasis.

Pezoporus wallicus – see *GROUND PARROT*

Phigys **LORY**
The single member of this genus is a beautiful small lory that has very rarely been kept in captivity outside Fiji. The Solitary, or Collared Lory (*P. solitarius*) has green wings and tail, and a ruff of elongated bright green feathers on its nape, from which the name Collared Lory is derived. Its forehead, crown and abdomen are deep purple, and the rest of the plumage is red. The iris of the eye, the beak, and legs are orange.

Immature birds have shorter feathers on their hind neck; their bill is brownish and the iris brown.

The length of this lory is 20 cm (8 in).

Found throughout the Fiji Islands, except in the Southern Lau group, the Collared Lory occurs in small groups in the vicinity of flowering trees, especially drala (*Erythrina indica*). It feeds on pollen and nectar. Common in some forested areas and the wetter, windward parts of Viti Levu and Vanua Levu, this lory is less abundant in open and agricultural locations.

In the past, the Samoans and Tongans coveted the red feathers of this little parrot, which they used for edging mats. Since the trade in these feathers was officially prohibited, wool has been used, but the demand has not totally ceased.

Export of this species and all other Fijian birds is forbidden. In the past, the few who were fortunate enough to keep the Collared Lory wrote of it in glowing terms. The British aviculturist Sydney Porter, who, 50 years ago, owned many rare and beautiful parrots, described it as "the loveliest and most engaging of the whole Parrot tribe."

Food, in captivity, consists of nectar and fruit.

This species lays two eggs. The incubation period may be as long as 27 days (25 or 26 would seem more likely) and the young spend nine weeks in the nest.

PILEATED PARAKEET
(*Purpureicephalus spurius*)
This parakeet is the only member of its genus. It is easily recognized by its mauve breast, bright in the male and pale mauve in the female. The color scheme is a most unusual one, especially the sharply contrasting tones of the male.

His ruby-red crown and forehead give rise to the name of Red-capped Parrot, by which the species is known in its native Australia. (The female's crown is brownish and green.) The male has lime-green cheeks, his dark green wings contrasting with his yellow rump and dark blue tail. The underside of the tail is light blue, tipped with white. The thighs and undertail coverts are scarlet. The male must surely be one of the most beautiful of all parakeets, whereas the female's colors are duller.

Immature birds are less colorful than females, with pale red and green feathers on the undertail coverts.

The tail is long and gives a total bird length of 36 cm (14 in).

This species, found only in the southwestern corner of Australia, is not common in aviculture, but is fairly common in the wild. It feeds mainly on the fruits of a certain kind of eucalyptus (*Eucalyptus calophylla*). Its bill has evolved its unusual shape (having a gap between the mandibles) to enable the bird to extract the seeds from the eucalyptus capsule. The curved lower mandible fits around the top of the capsule and the long upper mandible reaches inside to remove the seeds.

In captivity, Pileated Parakeets

relish the berries of hawthorn and pyracantha and, of course, branches of eucalyptus if available. If not, branches of fruit trees or pine should be provided, or damage may be done to the aviary woodwork. The diet should consist of the usual seeds and ample greens, such as chickweed, seeding grasses, sowthistle, and the unripe heads of thistles. Members of this genus eat more fruit than most Australian parakeets. When rearing young they require bread and milk, or a commercial rearing food, plus increased quantities of greens.

The clutch consists of four to seven eggs; the female commences incubation towards the completion of the clutch. Each egg is incubated for 19 or 20 days. On hatching the chicks are covered in long white down. This is replaced by gray down with a white patch on the nape, as in the other broad-tailed parakeets. The young spend about 33 days in the nest.

Although rather shy and very nervous, this is a most active and attractive aviary bird. It is also an enthusiastic bather (even recently fledged young will bathe) and a large, shallow water container should therefore be available.

Pionites – see *CAIQUES*

Pionopsitta PARROTS
The six members of this genus are small parrots from South and Central America, measuring 21–25 cm (8–10 in). Only one species, the Red-capped (*P. pileata*), is known in aviculture. It is mainly green, with dull red on the ear coverts; the bend of the wings and the primary coverts are deep blue. The male has a scarlet forehead and crown. This species originates from southeastern Brazil, where it is endangered by deforestation, and from eastern Paraguay.

Food should consist of a seed mixture (sunflower, safflower, canary, millet, buckwheat, wheat, and a little hemp and/or niger seeds) and plenty of fresh fruits and vegetables. When chicks are in the nest, corn on the cob and a rearing food must be provided. Only three or four aviculturists have had consistent success with this species; the most successful is surely Tom Ireland in Florida. The rearing food he uses consists of

whole grain bread, grated carrot, chopped endive, and vitamin and mineral supplements. He has found that the most successful method of breeding is to allow the birds to choose their own mates in a communal aviary. He then places bonded pairs in small suspended breeding cages.

Nesting commences in June. The clutch size is four or five eggs, and the incubation period is 21 to 24 days. The young spend about seven weeks in the nest.

This is a very sociable species, most likely to nest within sight or sound of others of its own kind. Its voice is pleasant – a soft warbling that could offend no one.

Pionus PARROTS
A group of small parrots from South and Central America, the *Pionus* are readily identified by their red undertail coverts. Most species are basically green, but two are unusual, one being dark blue and the other mainly brownish. *Pionus* can be very highly recommended as aviary birds and as pets. They are small in size, often have very gentle natures, and have quieter voices than Amazons or caiques, for example, making them very suitable to keep in the house. The size ranges from 24–29 cm (9½–11 in).

Pionus will accept a very varied diet, which should include plenty of greens and vegetables, such as spinach, kale, cabbage, chickweed, sowthistle, celery, carrot, and corn on the cob. Most will consume a lot

A Blue-headed Pionus Parrot (*Pionus menstruus menstruus*). There is sometimes a hint of pink on the throat or, in the subspecies *rubrigularis*, a larger pink area.

of small seeds, such as canary, buckwheat, and a little hemp. Sunflower and safflower seeds, peanuts, and pine nuts are also enjoyed. Favorite foods include cracked walnuts, spray millet, and hawthorn berries. All the usual fruits can be offered.

The plumage is alike in male and female and behavior can be misleading, so some form of sexing is recommended. Nest boxes should be in the region of 29 cm (11 in) square and 36 cm (14 in) high, or smaller for the White-crowned. The clutch usually consists of three or four eggs, but occasionally two or even five. The female incubates for 26 days and the young spend about ten weeks in the nest.

Easily the best-known member of the genus is the Blue-headed (*P. menstruus menstruus*), instantly recognized by the rich dark blue of the head and upper breast.

The rare and endangered subspecies *reichenowi*, from coastal northeastern Brazil, has a much paler shade of blue on the head, the underparts have a pale blue suffusion and the margins of the feathers of the undertail coverts are blue, not green as in the other subspecies.

This species has a very wide distribution, over most of tropical South America, so there is some variation in size and color throughout the range, but size is generally about 28 cm (11 in).

The next most frequently available *Pionus* is Maximilian's (*P. maximiliani*), which is mainly an olive-green with, of course, red undertail coverts and, according to the subspecies, purplish blue, dark blue, or vinous red on the throat and upper breast. In length it is 29 cm (11 in). Immature birds are duller and, as in most *Pionus*, may or may not have a band of red on the forehead. This species breeds well in captivity.

The Coral-billed (*P. sordidus corallinus*) differs from Maximilian's in its dark red beak, the inconspicuous area of grayish skin surrounding the eyes (white and very conspicuous in the Maximilian's), and in lacking the bronzy-green coloration on the wings.

The smallest member of the genus, the White-crowned (*P. senilis*), from Mexico and Central America, is occasionally available. It is recognized by its white crown, blue head, and size, which is about 24 cm (9½ in). This species nests readily and some pairs prove quite prolific.

The other members of the genus are more rarely available and more expensive. The Dusky (*P. fuscus*), from the northern part of South America, is mainly brown with the breast in various shades of vinous or brighter red.

The Bronze-winged (*P. chalcopterus*) is mainly dark blue with white and pink feathers on the throat and bright, almost iridescent, light blue under the wings. Imported birds tend to have a nervous disposition, and to overpreen each other's heads.

The exquisite rich plum color of the head of the Plum-crowned Pionus (*P. t. tumultuosus*) makes it extremely attractive. It occurs in the Andes of Bolivia and Peru and, as is usual with birds from high altitudes, it is not easy to establish in captivity.

The Massena's Parrot (*P. t. seniloides*), until recently considered a separate species, is the rarest in captivity. It differs from the Plum-crowned in having the feathers of its head gray and white. It originates from northwestern South America (Venezuela, Colombia, Ecuador, and Peru).

Poicephalus PARROTS

The range of basic colors found in the African *Poicephalus* parrots is remarkable. Sexual dimorphism is either absent or marked, and in two species the female is more colorful than the male. Young or hand-reared birds make delightful pets; as aviary birds they are attractive, and some pairs are quite prolific.

They could, perhaps, be described as the African counterparts of the *Pionus*, in that they are small (22–31 cm/8½–12 in).

A good variety of foods should be offered: soaked sunflower seed, sweetcorn, sprouted mung beans, peanuts, pine nuts, a mixture of small seeds (which the birds may or may not sample), plenty of fresh fruits and vegetables (including corn on the cob when young are being reared), and cracked walnuts. Cape Parrots are passionately fond of the walnuts, and they also like hawthorn berries. Bread and milk and/or a commercial rearing food, and even mealworms, will be accepted by birds rearing young.

Like some other African parrots in captivity, *Poicephalus* are usually winter breeders. In practice, this quite often means that the young have to be hand-reared; however, they then make totally delightful pets. Most species are small and quiet, which adds to their suitability as house pets. They are gentle and affectionate and may learn to repeat a few words. In contrast, many wild-caught *Poicephalus* are extremely nervous and suitable only as aviary birds.

Nest boxes for the smaller species should be about 23 cm (9 in) square and 60 cm (24 in) high. Boxes for the Jardine's and Cape Parrot should be about 28 cm (11 in) square. The clutch consists of three or four eggs and the incubation period is 26 to 28 days. Only the female incubates. The young spend 10 to 12 weeks in the nest.

For many years the Senegal (*P. senegalus*) was the only readily available member of the genus. It has long been one of the most inexpensive of the true parrots – partly because many adults are imported and these are difficult to sell, since they are extremely nervous. This species has a gray head, the upperparts and breast green, and the abdomen yellow, matching the brilliant yellow eyes.

Immature birds are paler and have a black iris, changing to gray, then grayish-yellow.

The voice of this species is not very pleasant.

Second in availability is Meyer's Parrot (*P. meyeri*). It, too, is reasonably priced. The size is the same as the Senegal, about 23 cm (9 in). Recognized by the yellow on the bend of its wings, thighs, and underwing coverts, the plumage is otherwise mainly grayish-brown, with the rump and underparts bluish-green or green. However, there are several subspecies that vary significantly; most have a yellow band on the crown, and the rump may be green or blue. Immature birds are much duller and lack the yellow markings.

Despite its dull coloration, the

Jardine's Parrot chick (*Poicephalus gulielmi*), one of the less frequently bred members of the genus.

Brown-headed Parrot (*P. cryptoxanthus*) can be recommended; the young birds especially make wonderful pets. Only 22 cm (8½ in) long, the plumage is mainly green, with the head dusky brown and the underwing coverts yellow. The eye is a piercing yellow. Immature birds have a brown iris. Like the Senegal, this species can be bred even in an indoor cage, with a minimum length of 90 cm (3 ft).

The unusually colored Rüppell's Parrot (*P. rueppellii*) is less often available. The male is an almost uniform dark gray, with contrasting yellow shoulders, thighs, and underwing coverts. The prettier female has the back, rump, uppertail coverts, lower abdomen, and part of the thighs blue. The iris of the eye is a startling red in adults and brown in young birds, which resemble the female but are slightly less colorful.

My own favorites are the Red-bellied and the Cape Parrot. The male of the former is exquisitely colored. (I can never pass the aviary of the male at Loro Parque without stopping to admire him.) He is soft brown above, with the lower breast, abdomen, and underwing coverts orange, and the rump soft green. All the colors are delicate. The beak and the skin surrounding the eyes are black, highlighting the red eyes. The female is very much duller, being soft brown, with the underparts and rump green.

Immature birds are like females, but the males have some orange feathers on their wing coverts and abdomen.

The only two species larger than

23 cm (9 in) are the Jardine's Parrot (*P. gulielmi*) and the Cape (*P. robustus*). Both have dark green body plumage, all the feathers of the wings being heavily margined with black in the former, whose head is green and black with the forehead orange, whereas in the Cape it is grayish or brownish (varying according to the subspecies), and usually only the female has orange on the forehead. The Cape is easily recognized by its enormous beak.

Both species tend to be nervous – the Cape Parrot exceptionally so. They do not easily adapt to captivity, and even captive-bred birds can be very shy. Tame birds are charming, however. This species is threatened in the wild, seldom exported, and reared in few collections. More effort must be made to establish it in captivity.

Polytelis PARAKEETS

The three members of this genus are large, long-tailed parakeets from Australia. Their elegant proportions, attractive colors, and tameness have long made them favorites with breeders. One disadvantage, however, is their long periods of inactivity.

They are very easy to feed, accepting a mixture of the usual small seeds (canary, white millet, oats, wheat, and a little hemp), plus sunflower seed and peanuts. Apple, carrot, spinach, or wild greens, such as chickweed, seeding grasses, and sowthistle should also be offered daily. Berries of hawthorn, elder, and mountain ash are relished.

Admired for its pastel colors and its renowned tameness, the Princess of Wales Parakeet (*P. alexandrae*) is known as the Princess Parrot in Australia. Its coloration is extremely delicate and unusual, and the two central tail feathers are greatly elongated, making up about half the total bird length of 45 cm (17½ in) in the male. The female has a shorter tail, slightly duller coloration on the head, and grayish feathers on the rump, back, and flanks. In the male this area is grayish-mauve. Both sexes have a pink throat, a pale blue forehead, and the upper parts soft olive green. The wing coverts are yellowish-green.

Immature birds have shorter tails and duller plumage than the female. The crown color is usually brighter blue in young males, who start to call and to erect the small feathers of the crown when several months old. Blue and lutino (yellow) mutations are being bred, but remain very expensive.

Although some pairs are good breeders, many are not, and thus the price of this species has never been low. Four to six eggs are laid and incubated for 19 days. They spend five weeks in the nest.

This parakeet is much better known in captivity than in the wild. Since in the wild it is highly nomadic and rarely observed, little is known about it, but it is believed to be declining. According to *The Atlas of Australian Birds*, only one breeding episode involving many birds has been reported since 1933.

The Rock Pebbler Parakeet (*P. anthopeplus*) is known as the Regent Parrot, or Smoker in Australia. Unusually colored, the male is mainly yellow with red and bluish-black in the wings and olive on the mantle. The underside of the tail is black. The female is olive green and has the underside of the tail feathers margined with pink. The bill is coral red. This species has the largest body size of the *Polytelis*, and measures about 41 cm (16 in). Immature birds are more like the female, although young males are usually of a yellower shade. Adult plumage is obtained by about 15 months. Breeding usually commences at two years.

This species is a very strong flyer and will make good use of a long flight area – at least 5 m (16 ft) in length. Some pairs will not enter a nest box, but will make a depression on the aviary floor (if made of soil or turf). As long as protection from the elements is provided, this nest need not be discouraged. Four eggs are laid and incubated by the female for about 20 days. The young spend five weeks in the nest.

The male Barraband's Parakeet (*P. swainsonii*) is an extremely striking bird with a yellow face bordered by a crescent of red. Its coloring and proportions are extremely elegant. The female is mainly green, of a less vivid shade than the male; the throat feathers are margined with pink, as are the outer tail feathers.

Immature birds are much like

the female, but have a brown iris – not yellow as in adults.

The clutch size is four to six eggs, the hen starts to incubate after the second or third egg.

Prioniturus – see
RACKET-TAILED PARROTS

Probosciger – see under *BLACK COCKATOOS*

PROTEIN, ANIMAL
Some parrot owners are at first aghast at the idea of feeding meat to their parrots, but animal protein in the diet helps to stimulate breeding in the larger parrots (such as macaws and Amazons), and protein for the breeding pair helps the production of strong chicks. Many parrot species are omnivorous in the wild and will consume animal protein if they can find it.

Having noted the enthusiasm with which many parrots will eat cooked meat, this is totally credible. They relish chop bones and a chicken carcass. Small, sharp bones should not be offered. Cooked lean meat left over from the table is recommended, and also filleted white fish, although fish is less popular than meat.

Hard-boiled egg is, of course, another excellent source of protein. To prevent waste, the whole egg can be chopped. If fed in quarters, for example, most birds will pick out the yolk and leave the white.

Insects are the protein most commonly consumed by parrots in the wild. Some insects are ingested accidentally (insects on nectar), but there is no doubt that many species seek out insects, especially when rearing young. At least one species, the little Golden-winged Parakeet (*Brotogeris chrysopterus*), regularly feeds on water snails, the bird's longish narrow beak enabling it to remove snails from the shells. The snails are stranded when the river level is low and are easily collected.

In captivity many parrots appear to seek live food when their chicks hatch. Australian parakeets, such as Rosellas and *Barnardius* species, have been known to dig up earthworms and feed them to their young. One pair of Barnard's Parakeets (*B. barnardius*) preferred chop bones to any other food when feeding chicks.

When parrots have young, mealworms will be consumed by many species of parrots – from small lorikeets, such as the Meyer's (*Trichoglossus flavoviriidis meyeri*) to large ones such as cockatoos. Cockatoos gnaw wood so avidly partly in their search for beetles and their larvae. In captivity, however, mealworms are too stimulating to offer to these birds before chicks hatch – possibly resulting in the male's attacking the female if she is less advanced in breeding condition.

Cockatoos will also consume maggots when rearing young, but great care has to be exercised to feed only maggots that have been cleaned for several days in bran. Any others are a possible source of botulism, a disease that kills countless wild birds and that has wiped out almost entire collections of captive birds. Some parrots also enjoy the chrysalids of maggots.

Live food, such as mealworms, appears to be essential for breeding Hanging Parrots (*Loriculus*); chicks die at an early age if live food is withheld. Ant pupae are also relished.

Aphids and blackflies would appear to be very small fry for medium-sized parrots, yet a pair of Meyer's (*Poicephalus meyeri*) were observed gathering these from a privet hedge growing in their aviary.

Psephotus PARAKEETS
This is a genus of extremes: it contains one of the parakeets popular with breeders and one that is shrouded in mystery – is it or is it not extinct? The Paradise Parakeet (*P. pulcherrimus*) has been the subject of speculation for years. The interior of Australia is so vast that it is perfectly possible for a species to be unobserved for some years, as happened in the case of the Night Parrot. On the other hand, claims that the Paradise Parakeet is in captivity are almost certainly fraudulent and perhaps the result of hybridizing.

Two species of *Psephotus* are common in captivity, the Red-rump (*P. haematonotus*) and the Many-colored Parakeet (*P. varius*), known in Australia as the Mulga Parrot. Sexual dimorphism is marked in all but one member of this genus. In the Red-rump, the male is mainly green, with the abdomen yellow and the rump red. The female is dull grayish-olive above and yellowish-olive below, with the rump green. The sexes can be distinguished in the nest, although a young male has less red on the rump than an adult.

There is an extremely popular yellow mutation in which the male is pale yellow, with the rump red, and the female is a pale creamy buff.

Red-rumps are usually prolific, and thus their price is low. Four to six eggs are laid and incubated by the female for 18 or 19 days. The young spend about 30 days in the nest, and their emergence is usually followed by the female's producing a second clutch. This species is renowned for its capability as a foster parent and can be entrusted with the young of any Australian parakeet.

These long-tailed parakeets have a total length of 26–28 cm (10–11 in). Accommodation and feeding should be as recommended for *Barnardius*, but the length of the flight area should be only 3.6 m (12 ft).

The Many-colored Parakeet male is a very colorful bird, with a yellow forehead, red on the crown, yellow and orange on the abdomen, and yellow on the shoulder and undertail coverts. The female is brownish on the head and upper breast and pale green below, with a little red on the shoulders. Immature birds are duller versions of the adults.

This species is a less prolific breeder; many chicks are lost because females cease to brood them at an early age. Chicks should therefore be checked first thing in the morning and again during the day, and removed for foster care or hand-rearing if necessary.

Both species have very pleasant voices and can be highly recommended as aviary birds. The other three *Psephotus*, the Hooded (*P. chrysopterygius dissimilis*), the Golden-shouldered (*P. c. chrysopterygius*) and the Blue-bonnet (*P. haematogaster*), are more difficult to breed and command much higher prices. They are recommended only for the experienced breeder.

Pseudeos LORY

The Dusky Lory (*P. fuscata*) is the only member of the genus. Its appearance and behavior are distinctive. The coloration is highly unusual – a blend of brilliant and subtle colors. There are two color phases. In the more common one, the underparts are fiery orange and black, there is orange in the wings, and the head and nape are orange, brown, and black. In the other color phase, the orange areas are replaced by yellow.

In both phases the upperparts are dark brown with copper and blue reflections, the undertail coverts are dark blue and the tail is bronze, blue, and orange (or yellow). The beak and skin at the side of the lower mandible are orange, and the iris of the eye is brilliant orange. It is difficult to understand how the Dusky Lory received its name – unless from an immature specimen – most young birds do have very subdued coloration.

In length this lory is about 24 cm (9½ in). The rump color varies; this is a sexual distinction in my experience, the rump color of the male being yellow and white, while in the female the color is more silvery.

The diet consists of nectar, fruit, spray millet, and corn on the cob, or sweet corn kernels. Bread and milk, or just milk, will be taken by some pairs when rearing young. A little sprouted sunflower seed can be offered after the chicks are about three weeks old.

The personality of the Dusky is extrovert. Fearless and noisy, some males become very aggressive when breeding. Dusky Lories are generally seasonal nesters, rather than continuous nesters like so many other lories. Two eggs are laid and incubated for 24 days by the female. The young spend 11 to 12 weeks in the nest. A nest box for this species should measure about 23 cm (9 in) square and 61 cm (2 ft) high. Nest litter should be changed at least once every week when chicks are in the nest.

Dusky Lories are fanatical bathers; they are also very hardy and will bathe during very cold weather. My pair used to enjoy playing in snow! In the wild they occur at altitudes as high as 2,000 m (6,560 ft). Very widely distributed throughout New Guinea, they are found in groups or quite large flocks. The flight is extremely swift and either direct or swooping. At Loro Parque in Tenerife (the Canary Islands), the Dusky Lory is the most spectacular liberty bird. A small group delights in passing among a crowd of visitors at immense speed and so close they may brush past the people's ears. The speed and accuracy of their flight, often swooping and swerving just above ground level, is a joy to watch. First to rise and last to go to roost, the sky may be completely dark when the last bird reaches its roosting tree. They will follow the keeper operating the electric cart carrying food to the parrots and can often be seen perched on the cart helping themselves!

Dusky Lories that are released in a suitable locality adapt immediately to a life at liberty, moving around in search of flowering blossoms just as they would in the wild. In such an acceptable setting, no species can be more highly recommended as a liberty bird. It must be remembered, however, that the release of exotic birds is illegal in many areas.

Psittacella PARROTS

These birds are virtually unknown in aviculture and seldom observed in the wild, because they are small, live in dense forest, and have plumage that provides excellent camouflage. Mountain birds, they are found in New Guinea from about 1,700 m (5,600 ft) to apparently as high as 4,000 m (13,000 ft). Few other parrots have been found at such a high altitude. They eat seeds, berries, and fruit.

Of the four species, probably only one has been kept in captivity. This is Brehm's Parrot (*P. brehmii*), the largest of the genus at 24 cm (9 in). The smallest are only 14 cm (5½ in). All members of the genus are barred with black and yellow on the mantle, rump and uppertail coverts, and also on the breast in some cases, and all have the undertail coverts red. They are sexually dimorphic, the female lacking the yellow band on the nape, but having the breast and/or flanks and side of the abdomen barred with black and yellow.

The members of this genus are likely to remain forever mysterious birds about which next to nothing is known.

PSITTACINE BEAK AND FEATHER DISEASE SYNDROME (PB AND FDS)

This is a viral disease that attacks the immune system, causing loss of feathers and abnormalities of the beak, and that makes the victim vulnerable to all kinds of further infection. In fact, it could be compared with AIDS in human beings. It is possible that more than one kind of virus is involved, as the disease does not follow exactly the same pattern in all species.

Cockatoos are the most likely to be affected and in these birds the disease is usually evident at the first molt. Prior to this, the bird appears to be in perfect condition. However, the new feathers may remain in the quill that also contains blood, or feathers that erupt will be deformed and soon break off.

The plumage becomes progressively worse, no powder down is produced, and possibly within a couple of years the bird is almost naked. The beak and nails lose their pigment and become soft and overgrown, and viral warts may appear on the feet. Alternatively, the beak may be unaffected. Some birds retain enough down to protect them from cold; others will need a heat lamp, because they will be unable to maintain normal body temperature – although ensuring that plenty of food is always before them will help.

Some birds with this unfortunate disease become very depressed; in

A Greater Vasa Parrot (*Coracopsis vasa vasa*), one year after losing all her feathers through psittacine beak and feather disease.

others morale and appetite are unaffected. A treatment that can slow down the pace of the disease has been developed. An autogenous vaccine is prepared using the sick bird's feather biopsies and beak scrapings. Weekly shots of the vaccine are given. However, only a few veterinarians have been prepared to do this to date. (Contact Dr. Cathy A. Johnson, DVM, 1970 Sciber Lake Road, "L", Lynnwood, WA. telephone: (206) 775 0121.) It must be emphasized that thus far no cure has been found – only a method of slowing down the progress of the disease. Affected birds can live for several years.

My experience with this disease relates to a pair of Greater Vasa Parrots (*Coracopsis vasa*) that had a few white feathers in their plumage when I obtained the birds. After about a year, the number of white feathers increased greatly and feather loss commenced. After another year the male was almost naked, but for a good covering of down, and the female possessed a few wisps of down and two or three primaries. These primaries were removed and examined under an electron microscope. It was found that a virus was present. In both birds beak and nails were normal, but the female had viral warts on her cere. When I moved from England to Tenerife, she was totally naked and had to be protected on the journey by placing a sleeve over her body, with part of a pair of tights placed over this to keep it in place. She traveled well, but suffered a little bruising.

Vasas are fanatic sunbathers and the warmth of Tenerife was much to the liking of the two affected birds. The female, totally naked, bathed with enthusiasm as soon as she was placed outdoors in the sun. The appetite and morale of both birds, one year after the move, seemed totally unaffected.

What to do with parrots affected with PB and FDS can be a dilemma. Not everyone would wish to care for such birds, or perhaps have the facilities (constant warmth) to do so. In that case one could donate the sick birds to an institution or veterinarian who is researching the disease, give them to someone who is prepared to care for them, or, as a last resort, have

them humanely put to sleep.

Psittacosis – see *ZOONOSIS*

Psittacula Parakeets

Long slender tails characterize the *Psittacula* parakeets from Asia. In aviculture the members of this genus range from the very well known to the extremely rare, from 30 cm (12 in) to 60 cm (2 ft), and from possessing the most subtle tones (as in the Plum-head) to exhibiting the strong color contrasts of the Derbyan. All

members of the genus are sexually dimorphic.

Unsuitable as pets, they are extremely attractive aviary birds. Accommodation requirements vary from an aviary of 2.4 or 3 m long (8 to 10 ft) for the smaller members of the genus, and also for the Ringneck, to a minimum of 3.6 m (12 ft) for Derbyans and Alexandrines. To display their beauty in flight, Alexandrines need an aviary length of 6 m (20 ft).

The diet is simple, yet varied. They require a seed mixture (sunflower, canary, oats, white millet, buckwheat, a little hemp, peanuts, and for the larger species, pine nuts), and also spray millet. The usual fruits and berries will be enjoyed, as well as greens (spinach, sowthistle, chickweed, seeding grasses, dandelion, etc.). A nutritious rearing food is essential when chicks hatch, especially when there are as many as four or five.

Many *Psittaculas* are early

A female Derbyan Parakeet, distinguished from the male by her black upper mandible and pink neck ring.

Rosellas

The Mealy Rosella *(Platycercus adscitus palliceps)* is one of the most distinctively colored of the Rosellas.

Brown's Rosella *(Platycercus venustus)* is the most expensive of the Rosellas.

The Stanley Parakeet, or Western Rosella *(Platycercus icterotis icterotis)* is one of the most popular and free-breeding of the Rosellas. A female is seen here.

Vasas

The Greater Vasa *(Coracopsis vasa vasa)* from Madagascar is probably one of the most primitive of parrots.

The Lesser Vasa *(Coracopsis nigra nigra)* is endangered by deforestation in Madagascar.

nesters, especially Ringnecks and Plum-heads, laying in February or March. Derbyans tend to nest later. The clutch size averages four eggs but can be up to six. Incubation is carried out by the female alone for 23 days in the Ringneck, and up to 28 days in the Alexandrine. The young spend about seven weeks in the nest.

The seven best known *Psittaculas* are the Alexandrine, the Indian Ringneck, the African Ringneck, the Slaty-headed, the Long-tailed, the Mustached and Derbyan.

Psittaculirostris – see under *FIG PARROTS*

Psittacus erithacus – see *GRAY PARROT*

Psittinus PARROT

The single member of the genus, the Blue-rumped Parrot (*P. cyanurus*) is a most unusual and distinctive little bird. It reminds me of a miniature *Tanygnathus* in some respects, and also of the genus *Psittacula*. Only 18 cm (7 in) in length, it is a quiet, rather inactive bird that must be difficult to observe in the wild. It is found in Borneo, Sumatra, Thailand, and the Malay Peninsula. Its status varies from common to rare, but it is widespread throughout the Malay Peninsula, including Singapore.

Although it has been exported fairly often, it has generally proved not easy to establish. In spite of its slightly hunched, top-heavy appearance, birds in good feather are extremely attractive. Above all, the voice is unlike that of any other parrot and decidedly pleasant to my ears. It makes a high-pitched piping sound.

Sexual dimorphism is pronounced in this little parrot. The male has a blue head and a red beak, whereas in the female the head is brown and the beak is black. In immature birds the head is green and the beak is horn-colored.

The plumage is otherwise mainly green and the feathers of the wing coverts are conspicuously margined with yellow, as in some *Tanygnathus* parrots. The prominent white iris of the eye gives the bird a rather mean appearance. This is quite appropriate where the female is concerned. As in some *Psittacula* species, she is dominant for most of the year and the male may be afraid of her.

The beak tends to become overgrown in some birds unless fresh wood for gnawing is regularly available. A wide variety of foods should be offered – all the small seeds, sunflower seeds, various fruits, elderberries, rosehips, hawthorn berries, chickweed, and other greens, small pine nuts, and peanuts.

This species has bred in captivity, but only rarely. Three to five eggs are laid.

Psittrichas fulgidus – see *PESQUET'S PARROT*

PURPLE-BELLIED PARROT
(*Triclaria malachitacea*)

The single member of this genus is notable for the male's thrushlike song; the female also sings, but not quite so expressively. A beautiful bird with large dark eyes, it is one of my greatest favorites. Alas, it is rare and difficult to establish in captivity. Originating from southeastern Brazil, it inhabits rain forest and woodland. There is no evidence that it is rare.

Sexual dimorphism in this species is pronounced. The male has a large patch of violet on his abdomen, being otherwise a rich and glossy dark green. The female lacks the violet patch. In length it is about 30 cm (12 in) including the

The Blue-rumped Parrot (this one is a male) is uncommon in captivity.

tail, which is long and quite broad.

Captive breeding, however, has rarely been achieved. Single youngsters were reared at Loro Parque, Tenerife in 1985 and 1988.

Purple-bellied Parrots in my own collection were fed on sunflower, canary, and niger seeds, peanuts, pine nuts, a small piece of spray millet daily, various fruits, the berries of hawthorn and elder, and corn on the cob. This species relishes the leaves and bark of freshly cut branches.

The clutch size is three or four eggs and the incubation period appears to be 28 days – a long period for a small parrot.

Purpureicephalus – see *PILEATED PARAKEET*

PYGMY PARROTS (*Micropsitta*)

The smallest parrots in existence, Pygmy Parrots measure only 8.5–10 cm (3½–4 in). The six species are unknown in captivity because they have proved impossible to keep alive. They are known to feed on small seeds, lichen, insects, and fruits – but the few that have been captured have refused to feed.

Their country of origin is New Guinea, and they are also found on the Solomon Islands. Their long toes, curved nails, and stiffened tail feathers are adaptations for climbing up and down the trunks of trees in their search for food.

These tiny parrots are mainly green, with contrasting colors on the head and breast.

Pyrrhura CONURES

Because of their loud voices, conures are not always appreciated, but the *Pyrrhura* species are different. Their voices are quieter; their plumage is intricate and in most forms extremely attractive; their personality can vary with the species and the individual bird. They are intensely inquisitive birds, and many become tame or fearless even though kept in an aviary. Ideal for breeders who do not have a lot of space, these conures will breed in suspended cages of 2 m (6½ ft) in length.

These conures originate from South and Central America. In all species plumage is alike in male and female. Their size ranges from 24 cm (9½ in) in *rupicola* to 28 cm (11 in) in the Blue-throated (*P.*

cruentata). The latter differs from all the popularly kept members of the genus in not having the feathers of the throat and upper breast (and the nape in some species) margined with white or buff.

The diet should be as recommended for *Pionus*, omitting the walnuts and pine nuts. This is an ideal group for the specialist, who could commence with the free-breeding Red-bellied (*P. frontalis*) and Green-cheeked Conures (*P. molinae*) and progress to some of those that are less well established in captivity and, in the case of the Pearly (*Pyrrhura perlata lepida*) and the White-eared (*P. leucotis*), are endangered because of deforestation. There are 16 species, nine of which are fairly well known in aviculture.

Some pairs prove very prolific. The clutch size varies with the species, four to six eggs in most, or eight to ten in the White-eared, Painted (*P. picta*) and the Rock Conure (*P. rupicola*). The incubation period is 22 to 24 days and the young remain in the nest for seven to eight weeks. The personality of hand-reared birds varies; *molinae* and *cruentata* can be nippy and unpleasant and decidedly aggressive towards other young birds, while others (including *rupicola*) are enchantingly tame and affectionate.

The Red-bellied and the Green-cheeked differ little in plumage – and more than one subspecies of both are known in captivity, adding to the confusion of identification. However, the Red-bellied has a narrow dark red frontal band, whereas in the Green-cheeked the forehead and the top of the head are brown, as is part of the ear coverts. The Red-bellied originates from southeastern Brazil, Uruguay, northeastern Argentina, and eastern Paraguay, whereas the Green-cheeked is found in the Mato Grosso region of Brazil, and also in Bolivia and northwestern Argentina. Both species are common in the wild.

Occasionally imported are the Black-tailed or Maroon-tailed Conures (*P. melanura*) of northwestern South America, and the Painted Conure of the Amazon basin and Guyana. (Imported birds come from the latter country.)

Pesquet's Parrot
(Psittrichas fulgidus)
from New Guinea –
the only large parrot
that never eats seed.

A miscellany of parrots (1)

Mexican Thick-billed Parrots *(Rhynchopsitta pachyryncha pachyryncha)* are endangered by the destruction of pine forests.

A male Blue-crowned Hanging Parrot *(Loriculus galgulus)* one of the most exquisite of small parrots.

The Black-headed Caique *(Pionites melanocephala melanocephala)* is found north of the Amazon, in the Guianas, Brazil, and Venezuela.

The Brown-headed Parrot *(Poicephalus cryptoxanthus)* is the dullest-colored of the genus, but young birds make most attractive pets.

Q

QUAKER PARAKEET (*Myiopsitta monachus*)

The Quaker Parakeet is well known for two characteristics: its ability to colonize countries outside its native continent, and for the fact that it builds a large colonial nest of sticks. Sometimes called the Monk Parakeet, its plumage is mainly gray and green, and its bill is brownish with a rounded upper mandible. The cheeks and throat are gray, merging into the pale gray breast feathers, which are tipped with white. Primary wing feathers are blue and black. In length this parakeet is about 29 cm (11½ in) including the longish tail.

This parakeet occurs naturally in southeastern South America (Argentina, Paraguay, Uruguay, Bolivia, and Brazil). However, feral populations have become established in parts of the United States and in Europe. These groups are derived from escaped cage birds or those that have been deliberately released by a birdkeeper who enjoys watching several pairs at liberty. They are so free-breeding that in some areas large populations have resulted after a few years.

They can be a menace to farmers because of their fondness for fruit and grain crops; otherwise it is a pleasure to watch them carrying sticks, building their nests, and fledging their young. This unusual nest building habit arises from the fact that some areas of open pampa, where these birds occur naturally, have no trees large enough to produce nesting holes.

In many areas, the Quaker Parakeet is the most numerous and conspicuous member of the parrot family.

This genus can be offered a wide variety of seeds, fruits, and vegetables, and also bread and milk and table scraps. Hand-reared birds make attractive pets and may learn to mimic. A colony aviary of Quaker Parakeets is a never-ending source of interest; the only disadvantage may be the continuous chattering and harsh calls that emerge from the colony.

At Loro Parque, in Tenerife, Quaker Parakeets abound. They build their bulky nests in palm trees. A nest that fell from a palm onto my terrace contained six chambers, plus two sparrows' nests. There is no lining, and the eggs are laid on the carefully woven twigs. The birds commence to nest in March. Five or six eggs are laid, but three or four seem to be the usual number of young to emerge at the end of May.

Some pairs breed again, so more young will be in evidence in September. Inevitably a number leave the nest prematurely and quickly find homes with the local Tenerife people, who will hand-rear them as pets. First, however, they have to be bathed, for they are generally crawling with red mites. Young birds are easily distinguished by their shorter tails, whiter skin surrounding the eye, generally more docile appearance, and bolder behavior.

Quaker Parakeets are ideal beginner's birds, being very easy to feed, hardy, and willing to breed. In an aviary they will use a nest box, or construct a stick nest if given a wire base and a large supply of sticks. Nest inspection is almost impossible, because a short tunnel leads to the nest chamber.

There is a rare and expensive blue mutation and an even rarer, more expensive beautiful yellow mutation of the Quaker Parakeet.

A Quaker Parakeet (*Myiopsitta monachus*) at its nest constructed from twigs.

R

RACKET-TAILED PARROTS
(*Prioniturus*)

These parrots are so called because of their two elongated tail feathers, each of which has a spatulate or racket-shaped tip. The shaft of the feather is bare. The racket-bearing feathers extend for 65–90 mm (2½–3½ in) beyond the length of the other tail feathers in the male and are shorter in the female. These tail feathers are molted one at a time. It takes six weeks for one of the tail feathers to grow, after which the other one will be molted and replaced.

Racket-tails, of which there are six species, are found in Indonesia and the Philippines. They measure 27–32 cm (10½–12½ in); one species, *flavicans*, is 37 cm (14½ in). Sexual dimorphism can be pronounced or slight, and coloration is pleasing – shades of green, with soft, contrasting colors on head or nape.

Members of this genus are rare in captivity, mainly because they are difficult to establish. Most die within a few weeks or months of capture. I know of only one bird that has survived for a number of years. A Blue-crowned Parrot (*P. discursus*), it was kept as a pet for at least 12 years by the late Fred Keen of Middlesex, England. It took three years to persuade it to eat anything other than cooked rice and raw egg. It eventually acquired a taste for cheese, the pips of pears, and crusts of bread.

If the opportunity occurs to keep Racket-tails, they should be offered plenty of fruit, the usual seeds, corn on the cob, boiled maize, peanuts, carrot, and bread and milk.

One of the most beautiful of the Racket-tails is the Golden-mantled (*P. platurus*). The soft green of the male's plumage is enhanced by small areas of pastel colors – pink on the crown, bordered by a patch of lavender gray, dull gold on the mantle, and lilac on the shoulders. The female is entirely green, and lighter below. Young birds resemble the female except for the central tail feathers, which lack the rackets, but have pointed tips.

This species is very rare in aviculture. However, in December, 1987, I saw it amid unforgettable surroundings. The Miami Metrozoo has undoubtedly one of the world's finest aviaries, called "Wings of Asia." Within its 6,100 sq m (1½ acres), it reproduces various Asian habitats – rain forest, swamp, etc. The spacious and natural surroundings enable the occupants to behave exactly as they would in the wild. Curator Ron Johnson told me that there was a male Golden-mantled Racket-tail within, but that we would be unlikely to see it as it was shy.

Eventually, a strange, almost unparrotlike call alerted us to its presence high in a tree. Then it flew down lower and perched amid surroundings so perfect I could imagine I was observing it on an Indonesian island.

Off-exhibit, yet within the confines of the aviary, another pair of Racket-tails are housed, and this male often visits the vicinity of their cage. If they breed, I believe they will be the first Racket-tails to do so in captivity.

RED MITES (*Dermanyssus* species)

Red mites are perhaps the most harmful and debilitating of all lice and mites that attack cage birds. Unlike feather lice, for example, red mites do not live permanently on the bird, but in cracks in the cage, nest box, or enclosure. The mites emerge at night to feed on the blood of birds, possibly causing anemia or the death of the chicks.

In a severe case, both nest and chicks could be swarming with red mites; in the dark environment of the nest the mites can live permanently on the chicks. If such a case is discovered, the chicks must be treated instantly, if feathered, by dipping them in an insecticide formulated for birds. Obviously the eyes should not be immersed in insecticide. On no account should they be returned to the nest box, which must be burned or properly sterilized. A new nest box should be used and a watch kept for any recurrence of the mites.

Breeders must be ever on the alert for signs of these mites: clusters of gray particles on woodwork or other surfaces are the

A miscellany of parrots (2)

The Blue-rumped Parrot *(Psittinus cyanurus)* is not well known in captivity. It is quiet in voice and personality. The head is blue in the male and brown in the female.

Above: Desmarest's Fig Parrot is typical of the genus of beautiful *Psittaculirostris* Fig Parrots from New Guinea.

Male and female *Eclectus roratus vosmaeri*. The female is distinguished from other subspecies by her yellow undertail coverts.

The Great-billed
Parrot *(Tanygnathus
megalorynchos)* has
the most beautiful
and intricate wing
markings.

feces of the mites. The mites themselves can be seen with the naked eye, and appear red after having fed on blood. Adult birds must be treated with a commercial powder formulated to rid birds of lice and mites. This can be obtained from pet stores and suppliers. Pyrethrum is a good deterrent.

After treating or painting woodwork in cages or a bird room, many dead mites may be found, and this can be the first indication many breeders have found that these mites are present. The use of a dichlorvos strip in a bird room will kill the mites, but care must be taken that the strip is the correct size for the room or area, or it could have a harmful effect on small birds.

Rhynchopsitta PARROTS

The feathered face and shorter tail distract one's attention from the otherwise macawlike features of the Thick-billed Parrot (*R. pachyrhyncha*) and the Maroon-fronted Parrot (*R. terrisi*). Some taxonomists regard them as subspecies rather than as separate species. They measure 38 cm (15 in) and 56 cm (22 in) respectively.

The Thick-billed Parrot is a most attractive shade of dark green. Its forehead and crown are red, and it also has a broad red stripe through the eye. The bend and edge of the wing and the thighs are also dark red. The underwing coverts are bright yellow. Immature birds have much less red in the plumage – this being mainly on forehead and forecrown. The skin surrounding the eye is whitish (yellow in adults).

This species has the most northerly distribution of any neotropical parrot. It formerly occured in southern Arizona and New Mexico, being an irregular winter visitor there until about 1930. It is not known whether it ever bred in the United States or was a visitor in times of food shortages only. More recently it has been found only in Mexico, but has nested within 150 km (93 miles) of the United States border. If it could be reestablished in the United States, this could ultimately prove crucial for its conservation, in view of the loss of its habitat and particularly the larger pine trees or snags (dead stumps) in which it nests.

Formerly the mountains of Arizona were the scene of ranching, mining, and prospecting; many men had guns and many Thick-bills must have been shot. Now the human population there is very much smaller and the habitat is excellent, with many potential nest sites in old woodpecker holes. Little timber-felling has occurred as the steep slopes make this difficult.

The large influx of Thick-bills smuggled into the United States in 1985 and 1986 (estimates vary from several hundred to over one thousand) produced the idea of reestablishing this species in Arizona. In September, 1986, the first release of 13 confiscated, wild-caught birds was made. On October 16 more were released. The resulting high mortality among these birds could have been avoided; releases coincided with the autumn migration of raptors that were more than a match for the less-than-perfect flight ability of some of the Thick-bills. Future releases will, it is hoped, be made with more care and this handsome parrot will again be counted as a native bird of the United States.

The Thick-bill is being bred in few collections; most private aviculturists consider it too noisy and destructive. However, outside the United States very few Thick-bills have been available and, at the time of writing, there was much controversy as to whether aviculturists in the United States would be permitted to keep these parrots because they are a native species.

The clutch size is two to four eggs and the incubation period is 26 days. In Europe this species nests late in the year (August or September) and has not proved prolific.

The Maroon-fronted Parrot differs from the Thick-bill in having the forehead maroon-brown, as the name suggests. The bend and edge of the wings and the thighs are brownish-red and the underwing coverts are silver-gray. It occurs only in northeastern Mexico, in pine forests, usually at an elevation of 2,000 to 3,500 m (6,560–11,500 ft).

Its population has decreased considerably in recent years, as its limited nesting area makes it a highly vulnerable species. The nest sites are holes in cliffs. Ravens have been seen entering known parrot nesting holes and are therefore almost certainly taking eggs or chicks. Also, the mixed conifer forests, on which Maroon-Fronted Parrots depend for food, are being destroyed by fire, logging, grazing, and clearing.

This species is unknown in captivity.

RINGING (BANDING)

Closed rings (seamless bands) are becoming of increasing importance in parrot aviculture. They are the only positive evidence that a bird has been bred in captivity. Much present-day legislation requires such evidence. A closed ring can be placed on the leg of a parrot chick only during the first few days or weeks of its life (depending on the species). If the ring is of the correct size, it can be removed only by cutting with pliers. If it is too large, it can still be removed when the bird is almost adult size.

Many breeders are reluctant to ring chicks because a ring can present a lethal hazard, and cause serious leg injury, or even the loss of the leg. The problem is that very little has been published about the correct ring sizes for the many different species bred in captivity. If the ring is too tight, the leg will become swollen. If this is not noticed, the result may be loss of the blood supply to the leg. Or dirt could lodge under the ring, causing an infection that also necessitates immediate removal of the ring.

If the ring (normally made of metal) is not sufficiently strong for the species, there is a danger that the bird could crush it out of shape so that it digs into the leg. If it is too wide, a callus will result. In choosing a ring, one must therefore take into account the circumference of the tarsus, the length of the tarsus from the hind toes, and the strength of the beak of the species concerned. The length of the bird is absolutely no indication of the correct ring size. Lories, for example, have much thicker legs than Australian parakeets of the same size.

Small parakeets (thin legs) can be ringed at an early age, about eight or ten days, whereas larger birds with thick legs cannot be ringed until they are about four weeks old in some instances. The age will vary in the same species;

not only is there individual variation, but hand-reared birds will generally be ringed later than those that are parent-reared, because their initial growth is slower.

If a chick is ringed too early, or the ring is too large, it will come off, not necessarily on the day following ringing, but up to several days later. If I believe I have ringed a chick too early, but know I will not be able to check the nest the following day, I push the ring up onto the tibia and move it down onto the tarsus a few days later. The ring is normally placed on the tarsus, but in fact it does not matter if it stays on the tibia.

The best instrument for ringing small and medium-sized parrots is a wooden toothpick; alternatively, a sharpened matchstick can be used. The ring is pushed over the three

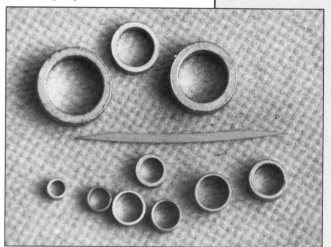

largest toes and the smallest one is then pulled through with the aid of the toothpick. With large chicks, like cockatoos and macaws, the ring is best pushed over all four toes, over the tarsus and up onto the tibia. If left too late, it can be very hard to release the toe of a large chick. In a difficult case, put a little petroleum jelly over the toes to ease the passage of the ring.

With some aviary birds, ringing is a hazard because the parents object to the ring and eject the chick from the nest in trying to remove the ring. In hole-nesting birds, where the interior of the nest is dark, this is not normally a problem. *Forpus* parrotlets, however, often try to remove rings. In one nest, a pair of *conspicillatus* were breeding for the first time. When the three eldest chicks were

Closed rings of various diameters and thicknesses. Those above the toothpick are 14 mm (½ in) and 18 mm (¾ in), suitable for macaws and cockatoos. The toothpick is used for putting the smaller rings on chicks' legs.

Bronze-winged
Pionus Parrot
*(Pionus
chalcopterus)* – an
unusually colored
parrot that is not
often imported.

A miscellany of parrots (3)

The female Purple-bellied Parrot *(Triclaria malachitacea)* is easily distinguished from the male: she lacks the purple on her breast.

Male Red-capped Parrot *(Pionopsitta pileata)*.

The Short-tailed Parrot *(Graydidascalus brachyurus)* is reminiscent of a miniature Amazon Parrot.

Highly intelligent and mischievous, the Kea *(Nestor notabilis)* is a mountain parrot from New Zealand.

No problems are encountered in ringing most parrot chicks in the nest. *Forpus* parrotlets are an exception. Two of the four Spectacled Parrotlet chicks seen here had their legs mutilated by their parents after ringing. One lost a leg as a result.

ringed, the parents broke the leg of one chick and so badly mutiliated the leg of another that the leg was lost.

Rings are frequently a danger in an aviary also, where the bird may become caught on a projecting piece of wire or even on a natural perch. I would urge all breeders to examine the interior of a cage or aviary with great care before placing a ringed bird inside. Also, when constructing cages from welded mesh, never turn back the mesh around the edges of doors, for example; always cut the wire off, leaving as little projecting as possible.

Technology of ring manufacture is improving, and the designs will surely become more sophisticated. A German manufacturer is now producing a smooth, extremely strong, plastic ring with no sharp edges. Numbers and letters, which can easily be read through the plastic, are printed inside; the desired data for imprinting is given when the rings are ordered.

Breeders must ring their chicks. Within a few years it is likely to be compulsory for the export of all parrots and for the sale of endangered species. Already the implementation of CITES is different for captive-bred birds. Closed rings are still the most effective way of identifying individual birds. This is of vital importance where the rarer species are concerned, to prevent the pairing of related birds.

All ring numbers must be recorded in an easily accessible manner – either notebook or computer. Perhaps the day will come when there is a central registry and the information recorded on a ring will be intelligible to all with a code book, as is presently the case with the Budgerigar Society in Britain, for example.

RODENT CONTROL

Aviaries, and the plentiful supply of food they contain, invariably attract mice, rats, and other vermin. To be rodent-proof, enclosures must have concrete floors, 9-mm (⅜-in) welded mesh, and no gaps anywhere in the construction – so very few aviaries are free of these pests. They consume and contaminate food, carry disease, and disturb and even kill the occupants and their young in the nest.

Every effort must be made to keep rodent numbers under control, or losses will be heavy. Poison or traps must be placed in boxes that birds cannot enter; however, it is pointless putting out poison unless all food is removed from the aviary every night. This is a time-consuming task that may not be possible in many instances, but little success will be achieved in controlling rodents unless it is carried out.

A successful and humane mousetrap is a box with a special flap through which the box is easily entered; once inside, however, the mouse cannot escape. Any number can be caught in one night. Those who dislike killing any form of life can then release the occupants – preferably several miles away, as mice seem to have a good homing sense! These traps are marketed commercially.

ROSELLAS (*Platycercus*)

Few genera of parrots are more popular with breeders than the Rosellas. Brightly colored parakeets from Australia, they are hardy and easy to care for and most are very free-breeding. They tend to be aggressive, so the strict rule is one pair per aviary. There should be double wiring between adjoining enclosures and, where possible, pairs of Rosellas should not be housed next door to each other.

These parakeets are recognized by the distinctive pattern of the feathers of the mantle and part of the wing coverts; these feathers are black in the center and yellow or red on the margin, according to the species. The length varies from 25 cm (10 in) in the Stanley Rosella, to 36 cm (14 in) in the Green Rosella (*P. caledonicus*) and the Pennants, including the long broad tail.

Rosellas do best in outdoor aviaries that are at least 4 m (13 ft) long. A seed mixture forms a large part of the diet and should consist of canary, oats, buckwheat, wheat, sunflower seed, and a little hemp seed in winter. Spray millet is relished, as are greens that should be offered daily and greatly increased when chicks hatch. The larger species will eat small pine nuts and peanuts.

During the rearing period a more nutritious food, such as bread and milk, or a commercial rearing food, is essential for good results. Rosellas seek a source of protein then, even consuming earthworms from the aviary floor. Apple, and occasionally other fruit, carrot, and berries are also eaten.

Sexing Rosellas can be difficult; generally speaking, males have a broader head and larger bill, and are more brightly colored. Care must be taken in introducing the male into the female's aviary (never vice versa); if he behaves aggressively it may be necessary to clip his wings.

The breeding life of these parakeets can be very long – up to 20 years and commencing at the age of one or two. Nest boxes should measure about 23 cm (9 in) square and be at least 60 cm (2 ft) high. The incubation period is about 20 days and the young spend five weeks in the nest. Clutch size varies from five to ten, according to species.

The most popular and inexpensive species is the Red Rosella (*P. eximius*), usually called the Golden-mantled Rosella, although this name should refer only to the subspecies *cecilae*, which has richer yellow on the margins of the feathers of the upper parts, and a greenish-blue rump – not pale green as in the Red Rosella. Both have a red head and upper breast, white cheeks and yellow abdomen – very colorful birds.

This is rivaled by the beautiful Pennant's Parakeet (*P. elegans elegans*), known in Australia as the Crimson Rosella. The cheeks, tail, and part of the wings are blue, the centers of the feathers of the back are black, and the rest of the plumage is crimson. The smallest of the genus is the Stanley, or Western Rosella (*P. icterotis*), a very popular bird, and sexually dimorphic. The cheeks are yellow, brighter in the male; his head and underparts are scarlet (patchy red and green in females and young birds) and the markings on the wings and back of both sexes are black, green, and blue.

One of the rarest and most expensive species, originating from the subtropical part of northern Australia, is the Brown's, or Northern Rosella (*P. venustus*). It is not easy to breed, partly because it chooses to nest during the winter months, and because there are often compatibility problems between male and female. For this reason, pairs should be formed when the birds are young.

S

SECURITY

Unfortunately, thefts of parrots, usually from outdoor aviaries, are common. All aviaries should be padlocked, and proper fittings should be used for the padlocks, not those that can easily be wrenched off or unscrewed. A covered run can be built around the entire perimeter of the aviaries, where a guard dog can run night and day. An electronic alarm system is very useful if the premises are never unattended. In this case, build the aviaries in a straight line to reduce the number of sensors required, thereby lessening the cost. The system that relies on a single infrared beam at each point is not recommended, because it will frequently be set off by cats and other animals. To prevent this, two beams should be situated, one above the other, so that only a human is likely to activate the alarm.

SEED

A mixture of seeds is an important part of the diet of most parakeets, conures, lovebirds, and cockatiels. It should be offered to large parrots – most Eclectus and even some Amazons prefer small seeds to sunflower seeds. There is little point in offering a mixture that contains sunflower seeds and a small amount of other seeds, as the small ones usually get lost and wasted in the bottom of the container. By offering them separately, one can control the amount and prevent waste. If small seeds are uneaten they should be discontinued.

Seeds such as canary and millet are best bought separately so that they can be offered on their own or in mixtures, according to the preferences of individual birds. If this is not possible, and there is a lot of waste, throw the discarded seed into boxes of earth; when the seedlings grow, place them, still in the box, in the aviary. The growing shoots will be eagerly devoured by most species.

An analysis of the content (for protein, etc.) of the various seeds could be misleading, as this can vary considerably according to where they have been grown, but generally speaking small seeds contain about 15% protein. Sunflower and hemp seeds have a high oil content, as do niger and linseed, which are more often fed to canaries and finches, but which make a useful winter supplement for any small parrots that will eat them. Canary and millet seeds have a high carbohydrate content, about 50% or 60%.

The staple components of most seed mixtures are canary and millet seeds. Canary seed does not vary significantly, except in size, but there are a number of kinds of millet. Panicum is recommended for lovebirds, *Neophemas*, Hanging Parrots, and Fig Parrots, and white millet for most parakeets, including *Neophemas*, Eclectus, and other large parrots that enjoy small seeds. Red millet is not used for cage birds. Spray millet is relished by almost all parrots, from lorikeets to macaws and cockatoos. Oats, groats, wheat, and buckwheat can be used to add variety to the mixture. Safflower seed can be fed instead of, or as well as, sunflower seed.

SEED, SUNFLOWER

Many pet parrots are fed primarily on sunflower seed, either through ignorance or lack of perseverance on the part of the owner. Sunflower seed, in moderation, is an excellent food, as it is relatively high in protein and other energy-giving nutrients, but if fed in excessive quantities, dietary deficiencies are liable to occur, notably of the minerals and vitamins that are found in fresh fruits and vegetables. Therefore, the sunflower seed content of any parrot's diet should not exceed 60%.

Several years ago, it was rumored that sunflower seed contains papaverine, which was said to be addictive. This is untrue. It was also believed to cause obesity, which was not borne out in an experiment carried out at the University of California in Davis (Department of Avian Sciences). In young cockatiels fed only on millet or canary seed for 60 days, the weight gains were greater than those fed only sunflower seeds for the same period.

I believe that providing sunflower seeds *ad lib* is harmful to the livers of small species, but I know of countless large parrots, such as Grays and Amazons, who have lived for many years on a diet consisting mainly of sunflower seeds.

This is certainly not to be recommended, but it quite often happens that someone buys or inherits a pet parrot (especially a Gray) that will eat no other seed

Sunflower seed.

than sunflower, which should therefore be offered sprouted. In this condition the vitamin content is increased many times; it is easier to digest and nutritionally far superior to dry sunflower seed.

I soak all sunflower seed before it is offered, partly to remove dirt and other impurities, and partly because it is more palatable after soaking. Simply soak in cold water for 24 hours, then rinse well before feeding.

The quality, as well as the cleanliness, of sunflower seed is very important. On buying a new batch of sunflower seed, it is advisable to test it for germination. If a seed does not sprout, it means that the germ is dead and the seed is of little nutritional value. About 90% or more of the seeds should germinate. I would consider 60%

to be a low germination rate.

The price of sunflower seed varies considerably according to the type; white is more expensive, since less is grown, but it is said to have a lower oil content. Seed that has been cleaned well is always more expensive. Cleanliness is of great importance. For those who do not normally soak seed, I would suggest that soaking be carried out initially to ascertain how much dirt the seed contains.

Striped sunflower seed is the kind most often fed to parrots. There are different types; the most obvious differences are in the shape and size of the seed. Look for a plump seed with a plump kernel. A long seed with a slim kernel is not good value, because the ratio of kernel to husk is low.

SELLING
Much advice is offered on buying birds, but the very important subject of selling is usually neglected. Birds are sold either through word of mouth or by placing an advertisement in an avicultural journal, or possibly a local newspaper. For security reasons, it is advisable to give a box or telephone number, but no address, in an advertisement. One useful practice is to give only the owner's first name, so that an interested person is unable to obtain the address from a telephone directory. This is wise in the case of very valuable birds. When describing birds in advertisements, state species (including scientific name in the case of something unusual), young or adult, sex if known, and method of sexing (proved breeder, surgical, or feather sexing).

Allow the purchaser to see the bird. Except in special circumstances, do not send off, by rail or air, birds that have not been seen before purchase. Instead, if possible, send a photograph of the bird or birds in advance, especially if of a rare species. Explain that the birds are sent at the purchaser's risk. Any physical defect, such as a missing toe, must be pointed out before the sale, and also the fact that this was taken into account when the price was calculated.

Worm Australian parakeets, and other species that are very susceptible to worms, a few days before purchase. Never carry this out on the day of sale, as the combined stress of worming and moving the bird could cause its death. Worming might also cause the bird to vomit in the buyer's presence. Explain the worming procedure to novice buyers.

Ask the purchaser who is traveling by car to bring a suitable cage or carrying box. Different species, unless closely related and small, should be placed in separate carrying boxes. Large parrots, even mated pairs, should not travel in the same cage or box, as the stress of close confinement might cause the male to attack the female.

The purchaser should be allowed to examine the bird in the hand.

Explain how the bird has been fed. Give the buyer enough of the basic diet to last one or two days, so that the bird is not faced with unfamiliar food as well as unfamiliar surroundings. If necessary, advise the buyer on suitable accommodation.

Establish whether the bird is being sold on approval, that is, whether you will allow its return for refund if there is a legitimate complaint. Some breeders will do this for the bird's sake, because they do not wish it to remain with someone who is not happy with it, or who may resell it to someone unsuitable.

SEXING, FEATHER CHROMOSOME

All birds have a chromosomal mechanism by which their sex is determined. Male birds have two Z sex chromosomes (usually called X) and females have one Z and one W. The latter can be identified under a microscope. Dr. Marc Valentine, a young American, pioneered the method of sexing birds using a blood feather (one which is still growing and therefore has blood in the shaft), which is removed from the bird to be sexed. The pulp is removed from the feather shaft and a cell culture is grown from the pulp. All that is required is one blood quill (perhaps two in a small bird), which must be kept sterile and must reach the laboratory within 24 hours.

After seven to ten days, enough cells have grown in the culture to enable a chromosome preparation to be made. The chromosomes are then analyzed, thus determining

sex, and also whether the bird possesses any chromosomal defects. For example, some birds are genetically intersex (neither male nor female) and are therefore sterile. Outwardly normal, this could never be discovered in any other manner.

Using this method, birds of any age can be sexed. Young can now be sold as sexed pairs as soon as they are independent. This is one of the most important avicultural breakthroughs ever made. At present, the service is available only in the United States, but it will eventually become the most widely used method of sexing birds.

An interesting spin-off of Dr. Valentine's work is that the study of heredity through the study of cells (comparative cytogenetics) can now be used to reveal evolutionary relationships of different groups of birds, or even, more rarely, those within one genus. Using the staining technique, known as C-banding, on 17 species of Amazon Parrots, Dr. Valentine discovered a commonly derived feature in Dufresne's, Festive, and Mealy Amazons, that is not ancestral to the entire genus.

SEXING, SURGICAL

Surgical sexing (by laparoscopy) is a service provided by many avian veterinarians in the United States and by relatively few elsewhere. The laparoscope is an instrument used in human medicine to provide an internal examination of various parts of the body. Used with a light source, it is an excellent means of examining birds internally, for diagnostic purposes as well as for determining sex. Species as small as lovebirds can be sexed with perfect safety, provided that a small-sized laparoscope is used.

So that the bird does not suffer, it is first anesthetized. There are two methods, gas (usually isofluorane) or injection. Gas has the advantage that after the mask is held over a bird's face, it is unconscious in seconds and (in skillful hands) is sexed and on its feet again in five minutes. The main disadvantage is that individual birds react differently to gas, and the correct dosage may be difficult to determine. When this method is employed, the owner is usually asked to withhold food during the previous 12 hours – or less time for a small bird.

When the anesthetic is injected, no food should be provided for the previous three or four hours. It may be several hours before the bird regains consciousness. During this period, it is wrapped in a towel that is lightly taped to keep it in place. When it frees itself it will be very unsteady on its feet for half an hour or so and should be kept in a warm room for the remainder of the day. The following day it can be returned to its aviary.

The sexing procedure is normally quite simple. Feathers are plucked from a small area behind the last rib on the left side. The area is cleaned with antiseptic, a small incision is made and the laparoscope is inserted. A light source and transmitting cable illuminate the bird's internal organs to reveal ovaries or testes. A vet can observe whether these organs are active and whether they are abnormal in any way, and also whether the bird is immature. In addition, a good view can be obtained of the air sacs, lungs, liver, and kidneys.

This should be a foolproof method of sexing adult birds in good health. On occasion, sex is impossible to determine, usually because the bird is overweight, or possibly because of some abnormality. A competent and reputable veterinarian will state if the sex is in doubt and make no charge.

Most mistakes are made with immature birds that are declared females when in fact they are young males. Some "mistakes" may be due to the fact that the owner has confused the birds. Parrots should be identified by a sexing ring or by a tattoo at the time of sexing. At Tenerife's Loro Parque, for example, a black ring is placed on the male's right leg and a gold ring on the female's left leg at the time of sexing. The ring number is recorded at that time.

If the bird is not given some mark of identification at the time of sexing, the owner should examine it carefully for some distinguishing mark – perhaps a missing nail, enlarged nostril, different coloration of feet or cere, abnormally colored feather that is replaced at each molt, etc. All owners should, in any case, keep a record card for each bird, with a photograph of the bird and a note of any distinguishing marks. This could provide the means of recovery if the bird is stolen.

After a bird has been sexed, it should be kept indoors for the remainder of the day. On no account should it be immediately returned to an aviary containing other birds. It may not be fully recovered and will therefore be vulnerable to attack.

The slight element of risk involved in surgical sexing arises mainly from the use of the anesthetic, not from the surgical procedure. Incidentally, some veterinarians will close the incision with a single stitch; others do not.

SEXUAL DIMORPHISM

Sexual dimorphism means that the male and female of a species are different in appearance. In parrots the difference is usually in plumage coloration and, in a few species, in beak coloration. In other species of birds there are other differences, such as size, color of feet, and even shape of the beak.

Sexual dimorphism may be subtle or slight. It is subtle, for example, in some Rosella parakeets (*Platycercus*), in which the male is a little more brightly colored than the female, as in the Golden-mantled Rosella (*P. eximius*). It is so subtle in some species that it may not be recognized. In Gray Parrots (*Psittacus erithacus*), males from the same area are usually darker than females.

In some species of *Psittacula* parakeets, beak color *and* plumage are different in male and female (as in the Derbyan Parakeet, *P. derbiana*), while in other members of the genus only the plumage differs. The male Ringneck (*P. krameri*) has a black and pink ring around the neck, whereas the female is all green (as are the young birds).

The Eclectus Parrot is the most extreme example of sexual dimorphism among parrots; indeed, few more striking examples occur throughout the avian world. The male is bright green with red under the wings, whereas the female flaunts a wonderful color scheme of red and mauve or red and blue – but mainly red.

None of the theories as to why

sexual dimorphism exists is satisfactory where the Eclectus is concerned. In most sexually dimorphic parrots, immature birds resemble the female, but in Eclectus there is no immature phase of the plumage. Eclectus can be sexed by appearance as soon as the first contour feathers appear at the age of three and a half to four weeks. It is not surprising that male and female Eclectus were once believed to be different species.

A less striking example of sufficient difference between male and female to be mistaken for two species occurs in a small number of the genus *Charmosyna*.

An unusual form of sexual dimorphism is that which occurs in one of the world's best-known cage birds, the budgerigar (*Melopsittacus undulatus*). The cere – the bare, rounded area of flesh surrounding each nostril – is blue in adult males and brown in adult females in breeding condition (pale blue or whitish blue in immature females or those out of breeding condition). In young males it is a pinkish mauve color. The only budgerigars that are difficult to sex by cere color are certain mutations, such as lutino, albino, and some pieds.

Inconveniently for the breeder, most parrots are either not sexually dimorphic or the difference is so slight as not to be recognized, or to be considered an unreliable method of determining sex.

SHINING PARROTS (*Prosopeia*)
The largest and among the most striking of all parakeets, the two members of this genus are extremely rare in captivity. They come from Fiji, where their export has been prohibited for many years. Deforestation is threatening their survival, as is the practice of removing all the larger trees, with a diameter more than 33 cm (13 in). This means that in some areas few trees remain with cavities large enough to provide nesting sites for Shining Parrots. These birds are not yet rare, but loss of nesting sites can cause a sudden decline in a population; this decline is then impossible to reverse because there are too few young birds.

One aspect of Shining Parrot care that does not present any difficulties is feeding. They accept an extremely wide variety of foods

– virtually anything offered. Fruits, vegetables, seeds, nuts, meat (raw or cooked), mealworms, and bread and milk are all eagerly consumed.

There are too few birds outside Fiji for captive-breeding to aid their survival and, in any case, the *Prosopeia* parrots are not easy to breed. This is more likely to be achieved in a warm climate, because they are in breeding condition for only a short time, and in Europe, for example, this is generally during cold weather.

One of the few European breeders found that the young were often killed, or died, within their first week.

One to three eggs are laid and the incubation period is 24 days. The young spend about eight weeks in the nest. On hatching, chicks have long silver-gray down, except for a patch of white down on the head, like *Eunymphicus* and *Cyanoramphus*.

The Masked Shining Parrot (*P. personata*) has very rarely been kept in captivity outside Fiji, where it is known only from the island of Viti Levu. It is mainly green with a black face, the center of the breast and underparts yellow, and orange on the abdomen. The iris of the eye is a penetrating and vivid orange. The beak is gray-black in

The Shining Parrot (*Prosopeia tabuensis*) – a rarely kept species from Fiji.

134

adults and paler in younger birds. In length it is 47 cm (18½ in).

The Red Shining Parrot (*P. tabuensis*) has several subspecies. *P. t. splendens* from Kandavu is distinctive because the head and underparts are crimson. There is a broad blue collar between nape and mantle. Wings and rump are bright green. The beak and iris of the eye are as described for *personata*. In length it is slightly smaller.

The other subspecies have maroon underparts and a narrow or wide blue band on the nape, or may lack this feature. A written description cannot do justice to the beauty of these birds. Their long, broad tails, majestic bearing and peculiar, smooth type of feather (in which each feather is not easily defined on the head, as in Eclectus) make them unique.

SHORT-TAILED PARROT (*Graydidascalus brachyurus*)

The single member of this genus is distinctive, although somewhat reminiscent of a miniature Amazon (especially the Festive Amazon, which is found in the same area). It originates from the Amazon basin (Colombia, Ecuador, Peru, and Brazil) and inhabits the flooded areas along the larger rivers. Quite common in the wild, this parrot is very rare in captivity, and captive-breeding has yet to occur. The females of one aviculturist, who lacked males of the species, laid clutches of one or two eggs. This species has a loud voice for its small size. Care and feeding should be as described for *Pionus* Parrots.

SPIX'S MACAW (*Cyanopsitta spixii*)

In appearance and behavior, this species, the only member of its genus, is quite unlike other macaws. It is the only bird classified as a macaw that has its head entirely feathered, in this respect resembling the conures. The coloration is unique – soft blue with the head pale grayish. In length it is 56 cm (22 in). The bill is black in adults and grayish-black with light markings in immature birds.

Known only from northeastern Brazil, the remaining small population had virtually been trapped out of existence by 1987, when it was rumored that the last three known birds had been caught. If another population exists, it is probably very small. This must therefore be considered the most endangered of all parrots from continental South America.

In 1988, about 20 Spix's Macaws were known in captivity. None was known except in Europe, Brazil, and the Philippines. Captive-breeding had occurred, but some years previously, and possibly in only one collection.

This macaw's extreme rarity, making it the most expensive parrot in existence, may result in its extinction. A Brazilian trapper can earn more from catching and selling one Spix's Macaw than in a decade or more of working. It is a tragic state of affairs for which there seems to be no solution at present.

In 1987, the very few holders of this species outside Brazil agreed to cooperate in pairing and lending birds. There is a good chance that captive-breeding will occur outside Brazil and no reason to suppose that this species would be especially difficult. The problem is that very few birds are available and they are scattered so widely throughout the world.

SPRAYING

Although bathing facilities must of course be provided for birds that do not have access to rain, these facilities are generally insufficient to ensure good condition of the plumage. Small birds may be able to bathe in the water container provided, but a thorough bath will be impossible for larger species. These can be seen dipping their heads in the water – sometimes obviously longing for a thorough soaking. This is best achieved by means of spraying. Buy a plant misting device for a small number of birds, or a large pressure spray for many. It is hard work using a hand spray if 30 or more need a soaking!

If spraying with warm water is a new experience, birds may object at first, and a light spray only is advisable. However, they soon learn to love it and become excited, ruffling their feathers, and perhaps anticipating the water by ducking their heads in the drinking water at the first glimpse of the spray. No conscientious owner will neglect this aspect of care; the birds derive so much enjoyment from it and their plumage acquires a wonderful gloss.

When drenched with water, the plumage takes on a leaden appearance in many birds. In those in which plummage is in excellent condition, perhaps after years of spraying, the water may just roll off, seeming hardly to penetrate the feathers or change their color. Moisture is essential if plumage is not to become dry and brittle; it also encourages a bird to preen vigorously.

In warm weather it is best to spray a bird outside, leaving it inside its cage if not tame or wing-clipped. Alternatively, the base of the cage can be removed and spraying carried out over a sink. The cage can then be cleaned to eliminate any accumulation of feather dust. (See *FEATHER*.)

STRESS

"Stress is the biggest killer of cage birds," wrote a British veterinarian some years ago, before most of us were aware of how true this is. Stress kills birds that are not 100% fit but that quite possibly would live for years with some condition that, under optimum conditions could be tolerated.

One of the advantages of hand-rearing is that it produces very tame birds, and such birds are not easily stressed. In contrast, wild-taken adult birds are extremely nervous and quickly stressed by close confinement or close contact with humans. There are no figures to substantiate this, but I would guess that the lifespan of a healthy tame parrot averages two or three times more, at the very least, than that of a nervous bird. Tame birds recover much more quickly from accidents or other traumatic experiences. They suffer little or no shock from being caught or handled; when they are breeding, inspecting their nest is more likely to produce aggression than a nervous reaction.

Other factors being equal, some species are much more susceptible to stress than others. As a very general observation, Amazons are not easily stressed, but Gray Parrots and cockatoos are. Nearly all cases of feather plucking are due to some form of stress. This is rarely seen in Amazons, but is very common in Grays and fairly common in cockatoos.

In some very rare cases, stress may have a genetic basis, perhaps because of inbreeding. I know of two examples in parrots that come from extremely small islands where continuous inbreeding has almost certainly occurred. The Uvaean Parakeet (see under *Eunymphicus PARAKEETS*) is very susceptible to stress, unlike the closely related Horned Parakeet. The habitat of the Uvaean is an area only 4 or 5 km (2½–3 miles) in extent.

The most easily stressed species that I have bred is the Tahiti Blue Lory (*Vini peruviana*), which also occurs on very small islands with very small populations. Regrettably, I have had numerous tragic experiences with such birds that I had hand-reared and that were therefore very tame. Usually, as the result of quarreling with another bird (although there were no injuries, or no significant injuries), a Blue Lory would be so stressed it would become comatose within minutes.

Only in a couple of instances was a bird revived. In one case, massaging the heart saved it; in another case, stimulating the heart with drugs given orally (not injected) failed to save its life.

So often birdkeepers subject their pets or aviary inhabitants to unnecessary stress; a little thought could avoid such situations. When catching birds in an aviary, for example, do so in a place (shelter or flight area) where as few other birds as possible will be disturbed. Do not worm a bird immediately after it has been caught – perhaps having been chased for two or three minutes. Put it in a cage and wait until it has quieted down and its breathing has returned to normal. Do not go along a range of aviaries worming the occupants if all the birds in the range can see what is happening. They will all be in a stressed condition as a result of watching other birds being caught.

Avoid sudden or loud noises. Do not startle your parrots by appearing without warning if they are unable to see your approach. Give some "contact call," such as a whistle or a word of greeting. Remember that any new or strange objects, even different clothing, can cause alarm, especially to nervous young birds that have not long left the nest.

T and U

SWIFT PARAKEET (*Lathamus discolor*)

The only member of its genus, this is a most distinctive little parakeet, unlike any other in appearance and behavior. Especially pleasing are its small beak, gentle and dainty appearance, and most attractive song (this word is an exaggeration in almost all other parrots except the Purple-bellied, *Triclaria*).

It originates from Tasmania, but in the winter it migrates to the Australian mainland, especially to Victoria, and in lesser numbers to parts of New South Wales and South Australia. Flowering trees are its main source of food. Like lories, Swift Parakeets feed extensively on pollen and nectar, and have a brush tongue for gathering pollen. This parakeet should be fed a varied diet, such as that provided by the German aviculturist, the late Josef Schumacher. He fed his Swift Parakeets on apple, orange, and soft fruits in season, such as strawberries, as well as sprouted seeds (sunflower, millet, oat, wheat, hemp, and niger), half-ripened wheat (stored in a freezer for year-round use), corn on the cob, and sponge cake moistened with honey.

Australian aviculturists are able to supply fresh branches of peppermint gum or white gum, in which the birds enjoy bathing when the branches are wet. They also relish flowers, such as fuchsia, which contain nectar. The Swift Parakeets at Loro Parque, Tenerife, greatly enjoy nibbling at the pine branches with which they are supplied regularly.

As aviary birds, Swift Parakeets can be highly recommended. They have delightful voices – incapable of being loud; they are not destructive, and they nest fairly readily. Three to five eggs are laid and incubated by the female for about 20 days. The young spend about five weeks in the nest. On fledging they are extremely pretty, with softer colors than their parents, dark eyes, and shorter tails. Bread and milk is a good rearing food for this species.

Tanygnathus PARROTS

Five members of this genus have been named; the authenticity of one is doubtful, another (*gramineus*) is unknown in captivity at the time of writing; the other three are interesting and very underrated in aviculture. Originating from Indonesia and the Philippines, they have not been frequently exported and comparatively little has been recorded about them as aviary birds. They range in size from about 31 to 41 cm (12–16 in) and have fairly broad tails of short to medium length.

These parrots accept a wide variety of foods. All the usual seeds, fruits, and vegetables, including corn on the cob, should be offered.

The most imposing of the genus is the Great-billed Parrot (*T. megalorynchos*), notable for its huge bill and for the beauty of its wing markings. The bill is generally slightly larger in the male; there is no sexual difference in the plumage. Widely distributed throughout Indonesia, there are eight subspecies with slight plumage differences. Immature birds have narrower and paler yellow margins on the wing coverts.

Quiet in behavior and voice, the Great-bill is unlikely to have a wide appeal. However, tame birds are delightful. A friendly male at Loro Parque attracts attention not by vocalization, but by bobbing up and down. He was received in November, 1987 at which time there was no report of this species having bred in captivity, and nothing had been recorded of its breeding habits in the wild. In January, 1988 the female at Loro Parque laid two eggs. This clutch was infertile, but from a second clutch of three laid in March, two chicks hatched.

A smaller version of the Great-bill, with almost similar wing markings and soft blue on the crown, is the Blue-naped Parrot (*T. lucionensis*) from the

Philippines and Indonesia. Its length is about 31 cm (12 in). Males are usually more brightly colored, especially on the wings.

This species is not well known in aviculture, but a few breeding successes have occurred. The two eggs are incubated for 26 days by the female. The young remain in the nest for approximately eight weeks. Gentle, quiet, and pretty, they are attractive aviary birds.

Adults of Müller's Parrot (*T. sumatranus* or *T. mulleri*) are very easy to sex: the beak is red in the male and white in the female, and also in immature birds. Müller's Parrot differs from the Blue-naped Parrot mainly in lacking blue on the head. It, too, originates from the Philippines and from Indonesia.

TEACHING PARROTS TO TALK

Many people are attracted to the idea of having a parrot that can "talk," that is, mimic. Many parrots will even say the right phrase at the right time – by

association. For example, when someone is making preparations to go out, the bird will say "bye bye," but parrots cannot normally be credited with actually knowing what they are saying.

To produce a good mimic, the three most important factors are a young bird, a suitable species, and a teacher who has patience. It is usually necessary to have a tame bird, or at least one that has accepted close confinement. An unhappy, nervous bird is very unlikely to mimic speech.

Although many species of parrots will learn to repeat half a dozen words, there are relatively few species that can acquire a sizable vocabulary. These are Gray Parrots, certain species of Amazons, Eclectus, and some of the larger lories.

Parrots can learn to "talk" from listening to other parrots, but usually the teacher is a human friend. To start with, choose a short, simple phrase such as "hello," "bye bye," or "come on." Repeat it at least three or four times whenever you pass the parrot's cage. In addition, have two ten-minute sessions of repeating the phrase when there are no competing distractions, such as television, and the room is quiet.

Most parrots are not capable of mimicking different voices but "speak" in the same voice, regardless of who has taught them. Grays and some Amazons are an exception; some of these birds are capable of reproducing the voices of several different people. Just as in a human child, the age at which they commence to mimic and the length of time it takes to learn words vary greatly from individual to individual. Some hand-reared parrots commence at an extraordinarily early age – even before they are weaned (small macaws, for example) – yet other hand-reared birds, even Grays, may not utter a word before they are nine months old. Parrots are capable of remembering phrases for years without repeating them; then something will prompt their memory.

Tepui **PARROTLET** – see *Nannopsittaca* **PARROTLETS**

Touit **PARROTLETS**
These small parrots, which

It is not generally known that the larger lories, such as this Black-winged Lory, are often excellent mimics.

measure from 14–17 cm (5½–6½ in), are virtually unknown in aviculture. There are two reasons for this: they inhabit the forest canopy and are therefore difficult to locate, and the few birds that have been caught have proved extremely difficult to adapt to captivity. They originate from South America and also Costa Rica in Central America.

They have a stocky build and short, slightly rounded tails. The beak is prominent, stout, and strongly curved. Most are sexually dimorphic, the females being less colorful on the wings and tails.

Very little is known about these birds in the wild, but their unusual beak may indicate specialized feeding habits, thus explaining why the few attempts to keep these birds in captivity have not been successful. Possibly only the Lilac-tailed (*T. batavica*) has been kept outside its country of origin – and on only a single occasion, to my knowledge.

Herbert Murray, from Essex, England, twice imported this species from Trinidad. On the second occasion, he received two adults and two young ones (caught together in a net at night). They had been force-fed in Trinidad. They would not eat seed, fruit, or mealworms, but existed on nectar plus a commercial food for birds. When the manufacturers ceased to make this product and another kind was used, three birds died.

This species is extremely beautiful, with colorful and unusually marked plumage. The forehead is yellow, the crown green, the nape feathers greenish-yellow tipped with black, the back brownish-black, and the wings, tail coverts, and rump are black. The tail is striking, the central feathers being violet and outer feathers mauvish-violet barred with black near the tip.

Food in the wild is known to include fruits, nectar, berries, seeds, and buds.

So little is known about the *Touit* parrotlets that immature plumage has never been described in some of the seven species.

One, the Golden-tailed (*T. surda*), from eastern Brazil, is endangered by deforestation. Another, a mountain-dwelling species from southwestern Colombia, northern Peru, and eastern Ecuador, has seldom been observed. This is the Spot-winged Parrotlet (*T. stictoptera*), usually found at elevations of 1,400–2,000 m (4,600–6,560 ft).

Trichoglossus LORIKEETS

Most of the lorikeets in this genus are medium-sized with longish tails, but several are small with proportionately shorter tails. Nearly all have barred markings on the upper breast. They originate from Australia, New Guinea, New Caledonia, and Indonesia. Some species occur in very large flocks.

In addition to nectar, fruit and greens, most *Trichoglossus* enjoy seed, such as canary and soaked sunflower. The amount should be greatly increased when young are being reared. One species, the Iris (*T. iris*), which is rare in captivity, needs a diet consisting of at least 50% seed and cannot live on nectar alone as the other species can.

Generally speaking, the members of this genus breed well in captivity and will rear several broods in one year; eight or ten youngsters in a year is not exceptional, although the clutch consists of only two eggs. The exception is the Perfect Lorikeet (*T. euteles*), which lays three eggs, or four on rare occasions.

The incubation period is 23 or 24 days and the young spend between seven and eight weeks in the nest. The smaller species will breed in a cage. One of the smallest, Goldie's (*T. goldiei*), actually breeds better in a cage than in an aviary. It is quiet, very pretty, and not destructive – in fact, the perfect bird for anyone attracted to lories but unable to erect outdoor aviaries.

One of the most prolific species is the Green-naped (*T. haematodus haematodus*), a very colorful bird and readily available at a reasonable price. It has more than 20 subspecies, whose identification can be difficult. Descriptions would be tedious, since the plumage is intricate and the differences subtle. Among the best known are Edwards's (*T. h. capistratus*), which has the breast mainly yellow, Massena's (*T. h. massena*), which has the nape brown, and Swainson's, or the Blue Mountain Lorikeet (*T. h. moluccanus*) from Australia, which is surely the most beautiful.

V

VASA PARROTS (*Coracopsis*)

The two species of Vasas are totally unlike other parrots in appearance and behavior. They are almost certainly the most primitive of parrots. Indeed, after studying them closely for three years (including the development of the young of *C. nigra*), I believe that they are the link between the parrots and the pigeons. (The latter family are generally accepted as being the nearest relatives of the parrots.)

They sunbathe like pigeons, their feathers are similar, and the young have very soft plumage; were it not for the shape of the beak they could be mistaken for young pigeons. The Lesser Vasa (*C. nigra*) has the extraordinarily short incubation period of 14 days – significantly shorter than that of any other parrot. No other true parrot develops so rapidly and leaves the nest so early – at about five weeks. At the time of writing, there was no published report of the Greater Vasa (*C. vasa*) ever having been bred in captivity.

Some aspects of Vasa behavior are unlike both pigeons *and* parrots. For example, the male has a loud and attractive whistling song. In the Greater Vasa *both* sexes protrude the sexual organs several centimeters when in breeding condition, the feathers on the top of the head are lost, and the skin turns yellow – really bright yellow in some birds. The normally gray plumage becomes darker in some birds in breeding condition and the beak color changes from gray to a pale horn color.

So much remains to be learned about this behaviorally fascinating genus. Their dull gray plumage will attract no one, but their pleasing personalities and unique behavior will appeal to the discerning and the conservation-conscious aviculturist. Vasas are found in Madagascar and the Comoro Islands, and the Lesser Vasa has a subspecies on Praslin, a very small island in the Seychelles.

Hundreds of Vasas have been exported from Madagascar since the early 1980s, because of the very severe destruction of habitat occurring there. Vasas will almost certainly be classified as endangered within a decade, so it behooves serious aviculturists to ensure that they are established in captivity before it is too late.

Immature birds resemble adults, except that the beak is dark.

The length is about 50 cm (19½ in) in the Greater Vasa, and about 38 cm (15 in) in the Lesser Vasa.

Vasas are hardy and easy to feed. They will accept a very wide range of foods. Some show a preference for small seeds; a mixture should be provided, including spray millet; walnuts and pine nuts are relished. A wide variety of vegetables, greens, and fruits should be offered.

VEGETABLES

Vegetables suitable for parrots can be divided into three categories: leaf, root, and other (such as tomato). A wide variety of leaf vegetables is acceptable, especially spinach, kale, and lettuce. Some of the larger species will eat cabbage, cauliflower and broccoli.

Among the most suitable leafy

Annual meadow grass (*Poa annua*).

weeds are sowthistle, chickweed, and young dandelion leaves. Great care must be exercised to obtain these from areas where spraying of pesticides has not occurred. No more should be offered than can be consumed in a few hours; unless placed in a container of water, greens soon become limp and unappetizing. Many kinds of grasses, such as annual meadow grass (*Poa annua*) and wheat are relished by a wide variety of species. Watercress is excellent. The owner of a single bird can keep a bunch of watercress for two or three days in a glass of water.

The most important root vegetable is carrot, which can be diced for smaller species and offered in larger pieces to the bigger birds. Some will not eat carrot unless it is placed firmly between the wires of the cage or aviary. Raw carrot is valuable for its Vitamin A content. Beetroot will be eaten by some parrots, especially if they start to receive it when young.

Other suitable vegetables are celery, tomato, zucchini, red and green peppers. Fresh corn on the cob is a universal favorite. It is advisable to buy corn on the cob in quantity when available, place them in boiling water for one minute, and then freeze them for use throughout the year. Cooking is not required, only thawing. Some small species, including lories, also relish the sweet corn kernels, which can be obtained canned or frozen. Apart from corn, only fresh vegetables are recommended. Peas in the pod and green beans are also very popular.

VETERINARY ADVICE AND CARE

Birdkeepers should not wait until they have a sick bird that urgently needs expert attention to search for a veterinarian in their area who is experienced in handling cage birds, especially parrots. In the United States, especially in California and Florida, avian veterinary specialists can be found. Elsewhere it can be very difficult indeed to find a veterinarian with experience or knowledge of parrots. Local breeders, a local bird society, or even a pet shop may be able to recommend a suitable vet, whom it is worth contacting in advance, stating that you keep parrots and may need advice in the future.

Do not fail to seek veterinary advice just because you are unable to find an avian specialist. Remember that all vets have laboratory services available to them. Fecal analysis usually provides useful information about a sick bird; the main problem is that analysis is relatively slow. It could be 48 hours or more before laboratory results are obtained, and an untreated sick bird is likely to die within this period. A parrot's metabolism is very rapid (the smaller the bird, the more rapid it is); heat, and usually treatment, must commence immediately once it is noticed that a bird is unwell.

Vini LORIES

Small lories of extraordinary appeal and beauty, there are five species of *Vini* that are virtually unknown in captivity. They originate from remote islands of the South Pacific and also Fiji. Their size is about 18 cm (7 in), and their plumage is mainly green or mainly blue, with shaft-streaking on the head feathers. Male and female are alike.

The *Vini* lories do best in planted, slightly heated enclosures. They do not easily tolerate low temperatures. Their diet consists principally of nectar and fruit, especially pomegranates, grapes, apple, and pear.

The clutch consists of two eggs that are incubated by both male and female for 25 days.

The Tahiti Blue Lory (*V. peruviana*) is an exquisite little creature. It is a glossy violet-blue, with the lower face and upper breast white. The orange bill and legs provide a striking contrast. Adult plumage is obtained at about six months, before which young birds are dark grayish-blue, with face and breast grayish-white and the beak brownish. This species is currently kept and bred in only two collections worldwide. (See *STRESS.*)

W

WATER

Parrots must have drinking water available at all times, and this must be provided fresh daily. The water container must also be cleaned daily or the water will become contaminated by the deposits in the container. Many parrots will bathe in standing water, so this fact should be borne in mind when choosing the water receptacle.

A few species (such as cockatoos) do not normally bathe in standing water, but they delight in rain bathing. In areas of meager or infrequent rainfall, aviaries should be fitted with sprinklers.

Careful thought should be given to the choice and location of water containers. Plastic hook-on cups are suitable for small parrots, and these can be placed at perch level or on a feeding shelf at a similar height. Heavy earthenware containers (such as dog bowls) are suitable for large or mischievous birds that delight in playing with anything movable. These can be placed on the floor (well away from perches where they would be contaminated with droppings) or on the feeding shelf. Cat litter trays make useful water containers in an aviary containing a number of birds.

Adopt a routine for dealing with drinking water during freezing weather. Empty all water containers at dusk; it is a lot easier than thawing solid ice next morning. Water can be prevented from freezing during the day by standing the container on cement blocks and placing a warming, candle, well hidden, beneath the container. However, this is only practical where a small number of containers are involved.

Automatic watering systems are available. They are very useful for large establishments where changing and cleaning water containers is a time-consuming task. Different types of watering systems have been marketed. One of them, to give an example, depends on a pivoting stem drinking valve. The valve has a protruding stem that is deflected when the bird touches it with tongue or beak, resulting in a flow of water. This ceases when the stem is released. The small quantity of water at the end of the stem attracts the bird. Because domestic water supplies have a higher pressure than that used in this system, a storage tank must be used. It cannot operate from tap water.

WINTER CARE

Special attention must be paid to the welfare of birds kept in outdoor aviaries during the winter. In cold climates there will be deaths that could easily be avoided if certain precautions are taken. Most parrots tolerate low temperatures quite well, but the combination of cold and wet conditions is unacceptable for many species, especially *Neophemas* and other small species that do not use their nest boxes for roosting. They are best housed indoors or in a bird room during the colder months.

Electric lighting is very important; small birds need to be able to feed for at least 12 hours each day. The energy obtained from the food helps them to maintain their body temperature in cold weather, and thus lighting is actually more important than heating. However, infrared lamps in the shelter will be appreciated by many species (see *INFRARED LAMP*).

Aviaries should be protected from wind. The best method is to erect plastic-covered frames around the enclosures. Drafts can literally be lethal. I was told of a pair of lories roosting in a shelter with moderate heat that were found dead, frozen to the perch, after an exceptionally cold night. The entrance hole to the shelter had not been closed and the lories had roosted in line with an icy blast.

Another winter problem is frostbite. Certain species (such as *Psittacula* parakeets and lovebirds) are especially susceptible. Birds that roost in the nest box will not be affected. Extra-wide wooden perches can be an advantage, as they push the birds' toes forward to be covered by the breast feathers. After a frosty night, perches must be checked carefully for signs of blood. Birds with frozen toes may bite them off, having lost all

Psittacula parakeets such as this male Derbyan are extremely susceptible to frostbite.

the intestines, feeding on the contents and depriving the bird of nourishment.

A low level of worm infestation could be tolerated for a long period, but the danger is that the worms will increase to the point where their host becomes thin and weak and the intestines are blocked or ruptured. The bird will die unless treatment is given before this stage is reached. It should be carried out at least twice yearly, before and after the breeding season. Even young birds can be badly affected, worm eggs having been passed to them in food from their parents.

A number of preparations are available that can be used for worming parakeets, most of which have been formulated for agricultural use, for far larger animals. Some veterinarians can advise on a safe dosage for parakeets and show the best method of administering it. If a veterinarian is unable to do this, advice should be sought from an experienced breeder, because administering the medication directly into the crop is the only efficient method.

Most worming preparations have a bitter taste, so that adding them to the drinking water is not effective; some birds will accept them if added to a favorite soft food. This is a hit-and-miss method, but it is perfectly safe.

It has to be admitted that many birds have died as a result of administering the preparation directly into the crop, either from shock or because the tube attached to the syringe has entered the windpipe or lung instead of the crop.

The alternative to worming all parakeets routinely is to send their fecal samples to a laboratory and then treat only those that are found to have worm eggs in their feces. This would be quite an expensive process, however. After a bird has been treated, the owner needs to know whether any worms are passed. This will be impossible unless the bird is caught and placed in a cage. The base should be lined with paper and the feces examined during the following 4 to 24 hours. Treatment must be repeated within the next two or three weeks if worms are passed.

sensation in their feet. Their toes or nails must immediately be cauterized to stop further bleeding. (The surgical cautery for birds sold by Phoenix Unlimited in the United States is highly recommended for this purpose.) Swelling of the feet is sometimes an indication that frostbite will occur if a bird is left out of doors any longer. If serious swelling occurs, consult a veterinarian, as a cortisone injection may be necessary.

All birds kept in outdoor aviaries should be inspected daily just prior to dusk. A bird that is sick or behaving uncharacteristically should be put in a warm place for the night. A sick bird would be unable to survive several hours of low temperatures. If you are unable to inspect your birds (including chicks in the nest) both at first light and just before they go to roost, do not keep them in outdoor aviaries. Keep them indoors or in an electrically lit outdoor bird room – or not at all!

WORMING

Some species are extremely susceptible to intestinal worms, the most common being *Ascaridia*. The most likely birds to be affected are Australian parakeets, cockatiels, lovebirds, and Kakarikis. These are all birds that like to search around on the aviary floor, where they may encounter the eggs of parasitic worms, from wild birds or other aviary occupants. If these eggs are ingested, they will hatch in the bird's digestive system and grow in

XYZ

ZOONOSIS

Zoonosis, or a zoonotic disease, is a disease of animals that can be transferred to humans. There are apparently over 100 diseases of animals that fall into this category, but it is chlamydiosis that triggers so much adverse publicity for birds in the media. This disease and Newcastle are the most important zoonotic diseases of birds. The latter may be found in poultry pathologists or laboratory workers. Symptoms are severe conjunctivitis or sinusitis.

Chlamydiosis is also known as psittacosis when found in parrots, and ornithosis in other birds. It is common in pigeons. In fact, a tourist feeding a flock of pigeons in London's Trafalgar Square or some other popular location is more likely to be affected than is the owner of a single parrot. Newly imported parrots, even though they have been quarantined, pose some disease risk, but the organism is also fairly common in budgies, and finches and canaries can also transmit chlamydia. The danger to parrot keepers, although real, has therefore been exaggerated.

Chlamydiosis is caused by an organism related to bacteria, *Chlamydia psittaci*. Feces are a source of the organism, which could be digested by other birds as a result of eating the feces; the bacteria could also be inhaled into the respiratory system. Whichever route is taken, when the *Chlamydia* bacteria reach the liver and spleen, they multiply. Symptoms in birds may include a discharge from eyes and nostrils, weight loss, and possibly diarrhea. The carrier of the disease may show no symptoms, but could infect many other birds.

If a diagnosis of possible chlamydiosis has been made, it is suggested that all birds that have been in contact with affected birds should be treated with antibiotics. Unfortunately, the treatment is very long, taking at least two months. It must, of course, be carried out under veterinary supervision.

In people, the incubation period of the disease usually ranges from five days to two weeks. Symptoms include fever, muscular aches, and respiratory problems; it may seem that the infected person is suffering from influenza. The main danger is that chlamydiosis will not be diagnosed and the patient will not be correctly treated. If the condition is diagnosed immediately, it will clear up in a few days with the use of tetracycline.